D1283010

FLASHLIGHTS
from HISTORY

A Brief Study in Social Development

By

JOHN S. FLORY, PH. D.

President Emeritus and Professor of English,
Bridgewater College, Author of "Literary
Activity of the Brethren in the Eight-
eenth Century," "Dramas of the
Bible," "Builders of the Church
of the Brethren," etc.

BRETHREN PUBLISHING HOUSE
ELGIN, ILLINOIS
1932

DEDICATION

To the Memory of Alexander Mack,
Founder of the Church of the Brethren

INTRODUCTION

To trace the growth of an idea, to follow the development of a community, to discover the forces that strengthen or weaken a nation, to lay bare the causes that unite or divide a communion—to do this well is fascinating and calls for sound scholarship, keen analysis and unbiased judgment. One must ever guard against the tendency to criticise too severely or favor unduly. To steer the course midway between Charybdis and Scylla is a most difficult undertaking.

In the story developed here the task was not always easy. Much of the material had to be dug from out of the way places. Often there were two sides to the question, the source material was meager and the records conflicting. To discover the material, give it the proper setting in a ȵeadable way, trace the growth of an idea and weigh correctly a religious doctrine or symbol call for the balance of the historian, the skill of the scholar and the integrity of the Christian man foursquare.

Dr. Flory is eminently qualified for just such an investigation. Descending from old Dunker stock he has given his life to promote the interests of his church, and has written several books dealing with her activities. He is conversant with her history, understands her doctrines, appreciates her culture and knows how she came to be what she is. He finds joy in telling the story to others.

The road which the Church of the Brethren traveled has not always been a smooth one. Born in the midst of deep-seated formalism, in a day when the right to worship God according to the dictates of conscience and the simple teaching of the New Testament was denied, this church has been a church of protest during its entire history. To adhere to the Master and his Word calls for protest against the devil and the world. This the church has attempted to do. The author shows how.

Part One deals with some of the causes that tended to divide the church. To those who passed through these periods the problems involved were vital. Unfortunately there were times when misdirected zeal was more powerful than cool judgment. Let us hope that a study of Part One may help us and future generations to avoid some of the pitfalls that beset the way.

Part Two paints a more glowing picture. Here we see the church unitedly facing her task, going forth to do her part in transforming the local community and in evangelizing the world.

If it was the misfortune of our fathers to see, now and then, a divided denomination, may it be the good fortune of our generation, or the next, to see these several divisions reunited, going forth as one united body offering to the world the time honored Gospel principles of the simple life, goodwill, peace, equality, temperance, brotherhood, belief in God's Word and absolute surrender to Jesus Christ the Son of God, the only hope and Savior of the world.

Elgin, Illinois.   J. E. Miller.

FOREWORD

The two series of articles making up this volume are presented as two groups of pictures, each of which portrays a definite line of social development. The pictures tell their own story. The history is that of the Church of the Brethren.

CONTENTS

PART I—DISINTEGRATION

9

PART I

DISINTEGRATION

CHAPTER I

THE CREYFELT EXPULSIONS

The flashlights in Part I of this volume are intended to bring into view certain conditions in the church from time to time which will help us to see the course the church has traveled. The pictures will be neither pleasing nor beautiful, but it is hoped that they may be instructive. If their lurid tints seem to be of the earth earthy, it will only serve to remind us that the church is made up of men and women, and that human beings are never perfect. The scenes are for the most part local, but they represent many parts of the Brotherhood. Each picture bears its own lesson.

Let us fix our gaze upon the city of Creyfelt in Germany in the early days of the Brethren Church.

To understand the significance of what we shall see, we will recall that Alexander Mack and the seven associated with him had organized the Church of the Brethren at Schwarzenau in 1708. From this small beginning the new body grew. The Brethren had a doctrine fully substantiated by the Bible and they zealously advocated their faith among their associates. In a few years a substantial body of members had been secured.

But they did not confine their activities to Schwarzenau. In their zeal to propagate the truth, they carried their messages into the surrounding provinces and only a few years after the organization they established themselves in the Marienborn district. A little later another body of members was gathered at Creyfelt, and almost at the same time a fourth organization was effected at Epstein. So within a half dozen years after the organization of the church four distinct bodies of members had been secured for the faith and the church was making itself felt in several provinces of the German state.

But now persecution began to distress them. It was two hundred years since Martin Luther had nailed his ninety-five theses to the church door at Wittenberg, and the churches had again become formal, spiritless, dogmatic and prone to persecution. They looked with disfavor upon all Christian bodies not definitely guaranteed state protection.

By 1715 the members in Marienborn and Epstein were driven from their homes by hostile governments. Many of these went to Creyfelt where for a time a reasonable degree of Christian liberty was allowed. By these additions and the activity of their ministers, the Creyfelt congregation grew rapidly and a strong congregation was built up.

Of this organization, John Naas was elder and Christian Libe was associated with him in the eldership. In addition to these elders there was an active body of younger ministers, Peter Becker, Stephen Koch, Henry Holsopple, John Henry Traut, John Henry Kalklosser and a young man by the name of

Hoecker. With this official staff of active ministers the Creyfelt congregation grew strong and influential and was making a deep impression upon the community. But just when all seemed so full of promise difficulty arose among the members themselves and completely wrecked the work so auspiciously begun.

The trouble came about in this way: young Hoecker, whose ministerial services were not required in the Creyfelt congregation, because of its large staff of active ministers, had been employed to preach for the congregation of the Mennonites in the city. He was well educated, a strong speaker and a man of fine personality and Christian character. For the pulpit services thus rendered the Mennonites, they paid him about two hundred and fifty dollars a year.

Among the members of the Mennonite congregation was a well to do merchant, who was also a minister, but one who preferred to devote his talents to business rather than preaching. In this family Hoecker occasionally visited. As the merchant had an attractive daughter, it is probable that she made the visits of the young pastor in the home of additional interest. In the course of events, at any rate, these young people became attracted to each other, fell in love, and were ultimately married, the father of the bride himself officiating at the altar.

But the bride was not a member of the church and so the marriage raised a storm of protest in the Brethren congregation. To many it seemed inconceivable that a member of the church and a minister at that would marry out of the church. All agreed that it was an offense that could not be winked at; so the matter must be investigated.

A council meeting was arranged for, and it is naturally to be expected that it was well attended by the membership. The matter was presented and considered at some length. It was clear that the sentiment was divided. Elder Naas, Peter Becker and some of the other leaders were disposed to deal gently with the young man, probably suspend him from the communion for a time and admonish him more fully of his Christian duty. But this kind of gentle procedure was not satisfactory to others of the congregation, so Elder Libe led a movement against the senior elder and those who thought with him and advocated much sterner discipline. Some sharp words were passed, excitement grew, and rash action followed. With the aid of four other Brethren, all of whom were unmarried, Libe so presented the matter before the congregation that they succeeded in passing by a majority vote a motion to expel Hoecker from the church. This was done and the congregation was left in a very distracted state of mind.

The meeting broke up in great confusion and many hearts were sorely grieved. Many of the members were not at all satisfied. Another council was called but resulted in other expulsions. It was taken up in later councils and still others were disowned. This procedure finally brought matters to a crisis. Elder Naas became so thoroughly discouraged and heartbroken that he told Libe what he thought of him and left Creyfelt. He moved up into the mountains of Switzerland so grieved that he was inactive in the work of the ministry for some years until Peter Becker later persuaded him to come to America.

The year following the Creyfelt disaster, Peter Becker organized a body of those who had been grieved and came to America, his party numbering one hundred and twenty-six members. But even moving away from the scene of trouble could not remove from them the terrible harm that had been done. The affair at Creyfelt was almost the only thing they talked about on the voyage across the ocean. And so discouraged had the members become and so crushed were their spirits that even after they landed in the new world, they had not the heart to take up the work of the church again for four years.

Hoecker himself took the matter of his expulsion very much to heart. He brooded over his misfortune, worried, fell sick, and finally died from grief and disappointment.

A pall fell upon the Creyfelt church, members lost interest, wandered away or drifted back into the world, and the church dwindled and finally ceased operations.

Elder Libe himself became inactive in the ministry. Later he gave up the ministry altogether and went into business, and finally himself married out of the church. The Creyfelt congregation once so full of promise was left a mere spectre of itself, a sad memory, a wreckage of shattered hopes and broken lives.

This division occurring within ten years of the organization of the church came near ruining the infant church. And how needless it all was. But the spirit of intolerance, always terrible to contemplate, did its deadly work. Self-will, dogmatism, and an intolerant spirit do not hear the voice of reason. Much less are they sensible of the wooings of the spirit of love, charity and forbearance.

CHAPTER II

THE SEVENTH DAY BAPTISTS

Not very long ago I stood by the grave of Conrad Beissel at Ephrata, Pennsylvania. Near by stands a plain marble slab that marks the last resting place of Peter Miller, and round about are many other plain stones which mark the graves of numerous others of the strange mystical band that took rise here and brought so much sorrow to the infant Church of the Brethren two hundred years ago.

On a little mound just beyond still stand some of the old buildings that bear mute testimony to the strange monastic community which once flourished here. First as the visitor approaches the group is a little log cabin, the hermitage of the founder of the Ephrata Community, with its large open fireplace, its small monastic windows, and low ceiling. Just beyond on the rise stands the Saal, or house of worship. Here are still to be seen samples of the penmanship once cultivated here and of the strange weird music in the minor key which is said to have produced such unusual emotional effects.

At right angles to the Saal and joining it at one corner is Saron, the sisters' house, or Cloister. The first floor was occupied by the older women. Here are still to be seen the means of their cloisterial occupations, spinning wheels for flax and wool, large hand looms for weaving, and the ancient pots and kettles dangling in the broad fireplaces where the cooking for the institution was done.

A steep winding stairway leads to the second floor, which was occupied by the younger women and where much the same occupations were pursued by the inmates. Along with the occupations already mentioned, basketry was certainly in evidence here. Here are still to be seen several of the large splint baskets about which some of our readers have heard. They are, it is true, too large to be carried naturally in and out of the doors of the little cell-like rooms in which they were made, but being without handles, it is a very simple matter to turn the baskets edgewise and carry them to all parts of the house.

A similar steep winding stair admits one to the third floor of Saron. This was the abode of the novices, the young girls who took upon themselves monastic vows and joined the society. Here is still preserved the furniture of the cell-like rooms which characterize the entire building. The little rooms are scarcely more than six by ten feet, and little higher than a person's head, with the couch built solidly into one end. This consists of a single board with a block of wood for a pillow. The little cell chamber is lighted by a solitary window, not as large as a single pane in the windows in most of your homes.

One leaves the building with a strange mingling of emotions. Here is still something of the middle ages set down in the new world, the ideal of monastic life, a belief that seclusion from the world is the means of saving one's soul. How strange does all this appear in the light of the plain teaching of the Master who gave his life in service to others and taught his followers to do likewise.

Across the little creek in the meadow another large building once stood. This was Bethania, or the Brothers' house, a monastery for the men. This has gone with the years but those still standing bear silent testimony to the quaint misguided enthusiasts who once lived here.

The story that lies back of these relics can be simply and briefly told. It is the story of the first division of the Church of the Brethren in America. It is a sad story, a story of mistakes and errors which has left in its trail a long record of sorrow and distress.

The leader of the Ephrata Society, or the Seventh Day Baptists, as they were officially called, was John Conrad Beissel. Beissel came to this country from Germany in 1720, a man thirty years of age. At that time he was so poor that a friend had to advance the passage money for his fare. He went to Germantown and worked for Peter Becker for a while learning the weaver's trade. Later he moved farther west into the Conestoga country. When Peter Becker and others from Germantown made a missionary tour through this country in 1824, they baptized a number of converts in Conestoga Creek, and organized the Conestoga congregation. Among those baptized was Conrad Beissel. In order that the little body of members might not be without religious services, the following day at the organization of the church Beissel was elected minister.

For some time all went well. Beissel was a gifted speaker, a man of winning personality, and the little church grew from the beginning. But in the course of time, the minister began to give expression to strange doctrines, which naturally spread discontent among the members. He showed a strong leaning toward the Old Testament. He declared the seventh day as the Sabbath. He seemed to prefer the Commandments to the Sermon on the Mount. He advocated a monastic order of life, denounced marriage, and advocated the celibate state.

Of course this produced unrest among the members of the Conestoga region. The leaders of the church at Germantown came out and tried to settle the matter, but Beissel hid himself away and refused to see them. When Alexander Mack, the founder of the church, came to America and learned of the situation, he made the long wearisome journey necessary to try to bring about a reconciliation. But Beissel would not consider the matter and refused to have any intercourse with the Brethren. This defection of Beissel grieved Eld. Mack profoundly, and the good man carried the sorrow of it as a burden upon his heart to his grave.

In 1728 the matter finally came to an open rupture. Beissel gathered his adherents about him, went down to the Conestoga Creek and there had one of his followers rebaptize him, signifying by this that he gave back to the Brethren their baptism and henceforth he proposed to go his own independent way. Then he himself rebaptized all who were willing to follow him into his new organization.

He now proceeded to organize his followers upon a monastic basis in which he recognized three classes of members: household members, or those who had married; solitary brethren, who took vows to live single, chaste lives; and spiritual virgins, who vowed to live pure virgin lives.

At first the little community grew slowly, but a few years later Beissel decided to move farther west, to the banks of the Cocalico Creek, where he established himself as a hermit and where his followers flocked about him in 1732. This is the beginning of Ephrata and the monastic system. Here in time, the buildings already mentioned were erected, and here the hermit system of life took its definite form.

Beissel now became active in building up his organization. He made proselyting tours among the Brethren churches and won away many to his cause. This brought great distress into various communities. Churches were divided, strong feelings engendered, and even homes broken up. But it was chiefly by proselyting among the Brethren congregations that Beissel built up his community.

Many influential members were led away by his mystical teachings. Among these were some influential ministers, Stephen Koch, Henry Kalklosser, George Adam Martin. Among these also was Ludwig

Hoecker of Germantown, the man who organized the first Sunday-school of modern times, the Sunday-school in the Germantown Church of the Brethren, in 1738. In less than a year after he had started the Sunday-school work at Germantown Hoecker joined Beissel. Alexander Mack Jr. also came under Beissel's spell for a time and for ten years led a monastic life. He later saw his mistake, however, and returning to Germantown, became one of the great bishops and leaders of the church in his later life. Another who came under the influence of Beissel's doctrines was the wife of the first Christopher Sower, who, leaving her husband and little son nine years old, took the veil and lived in the cloister for some years. Then on the intercession of her son who had grown to be a young man, she awoke out of the mystic bonds that bound her and returned to her husband and son as wife and mother.

So homes were divided, home life broken up, Brethren embittered toward one another, congregations rent asunder, well meaning persons distracted and confused, earnest hearts plunged into sorrow, and many hearts went down to their graves in grief because of the strange doctrines taught and the misguided lives that for a time flourished on the banks of the Cocalico.

And what has come of all this? Only the gray marble slabs and the weird old buildings with their haunting associations will stand as a silent testimony of the misdirected enthusiasts who lost sight of the plain teachings of God's Word in quaint fancies and wild, delirious dreams.

CHAPTER III

THE KENTUCKY BRETHREN

It may be that some of our readers are not aware that there was a time when the State of Kentucky was one of the promising fields of the Brethren Church; that here strong congregations had grown up under able leadership; and that here was exemplified a missionary zeal and spirit of sacrifice for the cause of Christ scarcely surpassed elsewhere in the Brotherhood. Yet for a hundred years the Church of the Brethren has not had an organized congregation in the Blue Grass State.

In this chapter we will review briefly the origin and status of two groups of churches which it is necessary to consider before we can understand the situation at this time and later. These two groups are the churches in Kentucky and the churches generally represented at Annual Conference.

The Kentucky Churches

Before the Revolutionary War, probably along in the sixties, Brethren from Germantown, Pennsylvania, began to settle in Kentucky. Among the earliest of these were Daniel Letterman and Casper Roland. Associated with these were John Hendricks, Giles Chapman, Joseph Rogers and David Martin, who had a few years earlier moved from Germantown to North

Carolina, but a little later joined Letterman and Roland in Kentucky. These formed a settlement in Shelby County in the northern part of the State and organized the members of their own families into a church.

These men were not adventurers or explorers, they were settlers. They had come to stay and to make homes for their families. Among them were able ministers and they were active in their ministry. They carried their evangelistic efforts into the adjoining counties. It was not long until other bodies of members were organized. They were strengthened also by migrations from other States which brought additional strong leaders among them. Among these were George Wolfe, Adam Hochstetler, Benjamin Hoffman and Francis Stump. Brother Stump was a descendant of Peter Becker and had lived at Germantown.

Under such leadership the Kentucky churches grew. Gradually they spread over Shelby, Muhlenberg and Logan Counties, and regions adjoining them. The churches grew in number and strength both by evangelism and migration.

Inducements were held out for Brethren to settle in the vicinity of these churches. A good climate and rich land which could be had cheap were inducements which appealed to many; so there was quite an influx into Kentucky from various sections, and some of the native people joined the church. As a result these churches became strong in numbers and in influence.

As many of their leaders had come from Germantown, they observed the ordinances of the church as they had been practiced there. And they reflected much of the liberal spirit that had always characterized the mother church in America. So they grew and prospered for more than half a century.

But these churches were isolated, they constituted a group among themselves. The members were poor. They had left their former homes to better their condition. It taxed their resources to establish their homes in the wilderness; but with all this they were active in carrying on such missionary work as they could do from their homes.

Thus isolated and remote from the main body of the church they had gone their own way and had prospered. They had grown, it is thought, to more than a thousand members in the Blue Grass State. And now, with the further migration of the Brethren, some of these from Virginia and Ohio began to come among them. And they were suddenly surprised to find themselves out of harmony in some respects with the practices of the church in other parts of the Brotherhood.

It was a surprise and a cause of sorrow for both the Kentucky Brethren and those from adjoining States to learn of the differences that obtained in the different churches. Both claimed the original authority of the church for their practice and neither was willing to concede fully to the other in the matter of church ordinances, because both thought that they were right. Out of this situation difficulties arose, but before considering these, let us look briefly at the other group of churches.

The Annual Meeting Churches

We have seen that the churches in Kentucky, because of distance and financial limitations, were not accustomed to be represented at the Annual Conference. Practically all the other churches of the Brotherhood were so represented. These churches migrating first from the neighborhood of Germantown, spread westward through Pennsylvania into Ohio. Another tide of migration went south into Maryland and Virginia. The minute book shows that the Annual Meetings were held as a rule more or less centrally among these four States.

In this way these churches were kept uniform in their practices, but gradually they had departed in some respects from the original order of observance established at Germantown. But these changes came gradually and in the course of time had received the sanction of the Annual Conference.

One of these that caused much of the difference was the method of observing the love feast. The Annual Meeting churches practiced the double mode of feet washing and did not place the supper upon the table until after the feet washing was done. They read a chapter between the supper and the communion and passed the salutation at the same time. The administrator broke the bread and passed the cup to the sisters. This had become the general order of the love feast and the Conference had given its approval to this method.

When Brethren from Virginia and Ohio moved

among the Kentucky Brethren and these differences in
practice became a matter of dissatisfaction, the Annual
Meeting of 1820 sent a committee to harmonize the
matter. The committee was not able to accomplish
much. Two years later another committee was sent
with but little better results. Other committees came
but agreement on the matters of controversy were not
reached. Finally in 1826 a committee was sent which
took up the matter and reached final action in regard
to the general situation. The action seems to have
been of a general character. Individuals were not dealt
with, but the Kentucky churches were declared out of
order and the members were given a certain period of
time to make their peace with the church. If this was
not done in the time prescribed they were counted no
longer members. Some, it would seem, accepted the
clemency of the church and were reinstated, but the
great body of the members were disfellowshiped.

Just how many these were has never been ascertained. Brother Abram H. Cassel estimated the number to be about fifteen hundred. This estimate is
doubtless too high. At any rate the number was
large, and the Kentucky Brethren were so discouraged
by the course of events that most of them moved
away into other sections, some fell away and gave up
trying to be Christians, while still others joined themselves with other Christian bodies. At all events the
congregations of the Brethren came to an end, and
there has been no Church of the Brethren in Kentucky
for nearly a hundred years.

When we look this situation squarely in the face,

the course of the church with the Kentucky Brethren does not seem justifiable. The whole controversy was over the ways of doing things. No principle of the Gospel and no doctrine of the church was being violated. Both groups of churches practised the teaching of the New Testament, both washed feet, ate a supper, and partook of the bread and wine. These were the events of the upper room.

This shows what may come from magnifying details out of their relative importance. When we lose sight of the Christ and his great message in the details of how he performed his work, we are in danger of rejecting the kernel for the husk. Jesus Christ and him crucified was a sufficient message for the apostles.

CHAPTER IV

THE FAR WESTERN BRETHREN

The Far Western Brethren were the descendants in large part of the disfellowshiped Kentucky Brethren. Many of those disowned refused to accept the verdict of the church but still accounted themselves members and went on with their church work. They preached, baptized, built up and organized churches. They scorned the idea that they were not members of the church into which they had been baptized.

Many of those who had been disowned in Kentucky moved north and west into new territory, into Illinois, Missouri, Indiana and Iowa, and here established churches. Among them were some very able men: John Hendricks, Isham Gibson, D. B. Sturgis, the two George Wolfes, Jacob Wolfe, Christian Shank and others. These men became real pioneers in the church, covering large territories on horseback, building up small bodies of members in widely scattered sections.

In a quarter of a century they had preached the Gospel from Arkansas to North Dakota on both sides of the Mississippi River. They were occupying new territory and seemed to be inspired with the mission of evangelizing the region that had fallen into their hands.

In the course of time the churches in the east had spread westward through Ohio and Indiana. These

were the churches that had been represented in Annual
Meeting and were therefore bound together by the
general decisions of the Conference. They were more
united in church polity than were the western churches.
Now in the course of the migration these two groups
of churches began to meet in the then far west. Of
course the difference in usage was much the same that
we have seen in Kentucky before.

But the main points in these differences may be sum-
marized. The Far Western Brethren used the single
mode of feet washing. The feet washing came after
the supper and before the communion. The salutation
was passed at the close of the communion service as
a farewell token of love. In addition to these matters
of church ordinance, the Far Western Brethren had
no order of dress, except that they dressed simply and
plainly.

The churches of the east, generally in touch with
the Annual Conference, observed the double mode of
feet washing, and the Conference had adopted this as
the order of the church. In these churches the administrator broke the bread to the sisters and passed
the communion cup from one to the other. In these
churches, too, the supper was not placed upon the
table until after the ordinance of feet washing was
completed, and the salutation was passed between the
supper and the bread and wine.

These differences in practice caused a good deal of
dissatisfaction and disturbance in those congregations
where the two usages met. About 1850, or possibly

earlier, an effort was made to harmonize the two parties, but at first little was accomplished. Several committees were appointed by Annual Conference to meet with the leaders of the Far Western Brethren with the hope of reaching a reconciliation. Nothing was definitely accomplished, however, until 1855. At this Conference a committee of eleven elders was appointed to meet with the leaders of the western churches. They met in the spring of the following year at a church in Adams County, Illinois, over which Eld. George Wolfe was overseer. Bro. Wolfe and a number of leading elders of the far west met with the committee and they worked out a compromise which went far towards a final adjustment of their differences.

It has been seen that most of the difference centered about the method of holding a love feast. As regards the single mode of feet washing, the Western Brethren were unwilling to give it up, as they claimed they were following the order of the Germantown church from the beginning. So they compromised by agreeing that when the Western Brethren were guests of those who, according to Annual Meeting decision practiced the double mode of feet washing, they would willingly concur in the same practice. But when the Western Brethren were among themselves, they should have the privilege to continue the practice of the single mode.

This decision went far towards a reconciliation. Four members of the Conference committee refused to sign the report, and there were still congregations that found it difficult to accept at once the recommendations of the committee

It was only four years later, however, until the matter was finally settled. At this Conference many of the elders of the far western churches wrote letters in a beautiful Christian spirit assuring the Conference of their earnest desire to be in full accord with the main body of the church and praying the Conference to accept them into full fellowship. After reading the many letters the Conference framed a statement declaring the Far Western Brethren in accord with the Conference and in full fellowship with the Brotherhood. This was in 1859.

This is a characteristic decision. Some of these members and the parents of many others had been disfellowshiped in Kentucky by general church action. Now hundreds of members converted and baptized by disfellowshiped Brethren and some who had never been held as members of the church were accepted into full fellowship by Annual Conference proclamation on the petition of a group of elders.

But if this action seems unusual let us see in it the anxious heart of the church reaching out to welcome into the fold those of like precious faith. True love is not abashed at being illogical. In fact the triumph of love and sympathy and forbearance over formal dogmatism is a higher logic. If the church ever made a mistake, in the long controversy over the Far Western Brethren, it was not when it opened its arms to them in love and reconciliation and union.

It should not be overlooked that the matters under dispute during this long controversy have been finally settled by the church almost entirely according to the contentions of the Far Western Brethren. Practically every item in their practice, the church of today has adopted as the usage of the Brotherhood. So these Far Western Brethren following the practices which the Kentucky Brethren had brought from Germantown were really the leaders in bringing the church back to the original order of its practice.

CHAPTER V

THE CHURCH OF GOD

This time our searchlight falls on a local congregation, the Bachelor Run church in Carroll County, Indiana.

This congregation had been built up largely through the instrumentality of two brethren. These were Peter Eyman (often incorrectly spelled Oiman) and Peter Replogle. For nearly twenty years these two brethren had labored in this rural section and had built up a flourishing congregation. Eyman was the first minister and the leading elder. About 1845 he became dissatisfied with certain usages of the church and was free to express his views in the pulpit and elsewhere. This caused dissatisfaction and ultimately the division of the congregation.

Among his contentions were these: that applicants for baptism should be asked the questions before going into the water, and that at love feast occasions supper should be on the table at the time of feet washing. He strongly favored the single mode of feet washing, and he opposed any restriction in the matter of dress.

Of course he had his followers. But there were also those who stood for the general order of the church in these respects. So the Bachelor Run congregation was divided in sentiment. Efforts were made to reconcile the factions but to no avail. As time went on the line of cleavage became more distinct and finally, about 1848, the factions decided to separate, part holding with Eyman, and the rest, under the leadership of Replogle, remaining with the church.

The division is said to have been effected in this manner: the members of the congregation met in a barn, a fence rail was laid in the middle of the barn floor; Eyman requested all who were willing to follow him to take their position with him on one side of the rail, the rest were to remain with Replogle and the church.

Eyman continued in the leadership of the Bachelor Run congregation and the body that remained with Replogle now called themselves the Deer Creek congregation. An irregular line was run so as to permit the members to live in the territory with their minister.

Now that Eyman and his followers were separated from the Brethren they proceeded to take another step and organize themselves into a separate denomination. At this point another young man begins to figure in the movement. This is George Patton, a minister in the Church of the Brethren. He now warmly espoused the cause of Eyman and his followers. He was present at Eyman's house when his followers met to form their new organization, and so interested was he in the proceedings that he was made moderator of the meeting.

One of the first questions to be decided was under what name the new organization would present itself to the world. Some scriptures were read and several names suggested. They finally decided to call themselves the Church of God. Under this name they started upon their independent career.

Although an official name had been adopted, the organization has been more frequently known by other names than that they had chosen. Probably more often than by any other they are known as the Oinmanites. They are known also as the Patton Brethren, and sometimes as the New Dunkers.

This body should be distinguished from another with the same name, the so-called Winebrennerians. While both are officially styled the Church of God, neither is generally called by this name. The latter went off from the German Reformed Church about a hundred years ago, and while they practice some of the ordinances very much like the Brethren, as trine immersion, feet washing, the communion, they have never had any official connection with the Brethren Church.

Soon after the organization their two leaders, Eyman and Patton, were very active in promoting their cause. They created a good deal of interest, not to say excitement, in the neighborhood. So keenly was this felt that the General Conference of the Brethren held in Wayne County, Ohio, in the spring of 1848, decided to hold a special General Conference in Carroll County, Indiana, in the fall of the same year, with the hope of reconciling the parties and bringing peace to the church.

This Conference met at the house of John Koontz

near Delphi, Indiana, on Saturday, the twenty-third of September. The following Sunday was spent in public worship, and on Monday a great love feast was celebrated. Tuesday morning the business session of the council began. The matter was gone into and found to be as we have stated it. The meeting resulted in much good. Some of those who had gone away from the church asked pardon and were reinstated. Others who were uncertain and confused were restored to peace and tranquillity. But it was too late to effect a complete reconciliation. The organization of the new body had already been effected, as we have seen.

Because of the importance of this case, it having occasioned a special General Conference to consider it, I will insert the decision arrived at by the Conference:

" In regard to the difficulties of the Bachelor Run church with Brothers Oyman and Patton and others, the Brethren in general council considered that there had been committed errors on both sides, in consequence of which many members of both sides made satisfactory acknowledgements before the meeting, and it was concluded that with such, all that is past should be forgiven and forgotten, and with as many as may come and make satisfaction, and that they should all be received in the full fellowship and Brother David Fisher in his office as speaker. Furthermore this meeting considers and counsels that Brothers Oyman and Patton, and such others that hold with them, should yet have time to reflect and should they come, also, in a reasonable space of time and make satisfactory acknowledgement then the church should also forgive them. But if they should persist in their contrary course, going on holding meetings in opposition to the church, there would be no other way but to put them in full avoidance according to First Corinthians 5."

The clemency held out to Eyman and Patton was not accepted, and at a later council of the church they were disowned. They now gave themselves to building up their independent organization. They changed their church polity so as to accommodate the practices for which they had contended. Among the more important of these were the following: they adopted as a form of baptism single backward immersion. At the communion service they retained the table but no supper. They adopted the open communion and repudiated the doctrines of nonconformity, non-secrecy, and non-litigation.

Not very long after the organization was made Eyman died, leaving Patton as the leading elder. Although he was a man of ability and very zealous, the body grew but slowly. They built their first church house in 1872. In the three quarters of a century since the organization, they have established themselves in some half dozen counties in eastern Indiana and a few are found at other places. In 1928 Dr. Carroll, the church statistician, gave their total membership as eleven hundred.

And in this consists the tragedy of such movements. A small group of members like this cannot put on a program of aggressive Christian work. They are too weak financially to establish and maintain missions in the heathen world, and they cannot support and develop educational and philanthropic institutions through which they can make their impress upon their contemporaries. Their energies are exhausted in keeping alive the feeble establishments they have set up. Any body of Christians that does not have a message for the world will sooner or later find itself without a mission for itself.

CHAPTER VI

THE CONGREGATIONAL BRETHREN AND THE LEEDY BRETHREN

The Congregational Brethren

This time we shall consider briefly two small bodies because there are certain resemblances in their history and they come to a common end. A factor in the origin of each of these bodies was that time-old question of how the ordinance of feet washing should be conducted, and details of the communion.

The Congregational Brethren were mainly the left-overs of the Far Western Brethren when they were received back into the church. We have already seen that when the Conference of 1859 proclaimed the Far Western Brethren in full fellowship with the church there were some who found it difficult to adapt themselves to the conditions and therefore continued the agitation of the question.

The point on which they could not be reconciled was that the church as a body still practiced and held to the double mode of feet washing. While the western churches had been granted the privilege of practicing the single mode when they were among themselves, they looked upon this purely as a compromise and as a matter of expediency, while they regarded the question in controversy a matter of principle. They felt sure that the single mode was the right and the only right way of administering the ordinance. They therefore refused to accept the invitation of the Conference to full membership of the church and so continued their agitation.

This condition led to other committees being sent to the churches where the difficulty prevailed. These were chiefly in Missouri and Illinois. During the years that followed several committees were sent but without accomplishing much. Finally in 1872 several elders with a number of ministers and a considerable number of members were expelled. A few ministers were also silenced.

Among these were very influential members. One was the son of Eld. Isham Gibson of Illinois who had done such a wonderful pioneer work in this new country in company with Eld. George Wolfe. Among them were also two sons of Eld. John Hendricks who had been a great leader and preacher in Kentucky and Tennessee and later in Illinois and Missouri. These men had a following and when they were put out of the church there were strong bodies of members to go with them.

After their expulsion these ministers went on preaching and baptizing as before. They taught and practiced all the doctrines of the Brethren and varied from them only in the manner of the observance of feet washing. Instead of organizing themselves into an independent body they simply went on, each church managing its own affairs and being bound together only by the circumstances of their condition and their unity and faith in the Gospel. They really became congregational and from this fact originated the name by which they were known.

They never became numerous although their leaders were active and capable; and when the Progressives in 1883 proposed a union with them, they joined as a body in the formation of the new organization, the Brethren Church.

It may not be inappropriate to point out here that the doctrine these Brethren contended for so stoutly and for which they allowed themselves to be disfellowshiped from the church they loved, the mother church, has since been accepted in full and made the universal practice of the denomination.

The Leedy Brethren

Members by the name of Leedy moved from Bedford County, Pennsylvania, to Knox County, Ohio, about the beginning of the nineteenth century. A few years later, the Owl Creek congregation was organized, mostly from Leedy families. The church grew through the years and became strong. For half a century there was nothing to bring this church or its people especially into prominence, until along in the 50's when the order of feet washing was being discussed all over the Brotherhood. The Owl Creek church took up the question, as many other congregations had done, and voted in favor of the single mode, thus aligning themselves with the Far Western Brethren. Yet here they were in Ohio in the midst of the Annual Meeting churches and the Annual Meeting had declared in

favor of the double mode. So they were clearly out
of order. An Annual Meeting committee was sent
as was the custom in that day.

The Leedys undertook to defend their course and
to prove their contention by the Scriptures. They also
believed they had the authority of the church from the
beginning in substantiation of their position. These
things, however, did not convince the committee, and
as a result, a number of them were disfellowshiped.
Among them were several elders and a number of
ministers. As they naturally had their friends and
followers, a considerable body, besides those expelled,
threw in their lot with them.

As many of those who had been disowned or left
the church were of the one name, they came to be
known generally as the Leedy Brethren. I have not
discovered any evidence to show that they formally
incorporated themselves under this or any other name.
But many of them were prominent, had been old settlers, had grown into the community life, and were
held in high esteem because of their character and
ability. So the names of their leaders naturally at-
tached itself to them. The Leedy Brethren in Ohio
did much as the Hendrickses and Gibsons did in Missouri and Illinois. They went on with their church
work, continued preaching and baptizing converts and
held their membership together and at work.

The time when this action was taken by the Annual
Meeting committee was in September, 1858. The next
June, it will be remembered, was the time when the

Annual Meeting received back into fellowship the Far Western Brethren along with their single mode of feet washing; but that was too late to meet the conditions at Owl Creek. They continued to go on their own way until they too received the invitation from the Progressives in 1883 to join them in the formation of a new denomination. This they decided to do and in the Dayton assembly, June, 1883, the Leedy Brethren together with the Progressives and the Congregational Brethren joined in the formation of the Brethren Church.

These two bodies have a unique history. They both lost their membership in the mother church because of a doctrine that they held more dear than membership in the church. The fact that these experiences were occurring repeatedly indicates that there was a need in the church of some change in its policy of dealing with members who out of conscientious scruples saw differently from what the church had taught.

It must be a great satisfaction to all who love the church and her doctrines to know that the church did have within itself the power and wisdom to modify its methods so that without sacrificing any principle it could give to every member a free exercise of conscience and at the same time preserve in dignity the principles of the Gospel.

CHAPTER VII

THE JOHN A. BOWMAN BRETHREN AND THE HONITES

Our picture today will be revealed by two snapshots. These will take us to the mountains of Tennessee and the plains of Kentucky and Ohio. There is not much that is common in these two stories. In fact they are contrasts rather than parallels, but they are brought together here with the idea of helping us see more clearly and concretely the vision that these flashlights are intended to reveal.

The John A. Bowman Brethren

This story centers in the Pleasant Hill congregation in Eastern Tennessee. John A. Bowman was an elder in this congregation and one of the leading elders of the Tennessee District. While largely a self-made man, he was a strong preacher, a man of unimpeachable integrity of character, and one universally beloved by those who knew him. He was one of the prominent elders of the south in this day.

It was along about 1857 that he had been appointed by the court as executor of an estate. It happened in the course of his official duty that it became necessary for him to bring suit in chancery in order to close up the business. Before doing this, however, he took counsel of the church and the church gave him permission to use the law as the case required. The estate was settled up, apparently to the satisfaction of everybody concerned.

Some time later, however, some of the interested parties became dissatisfied. They brought charges against the administrator and the matter ultimately got into the church. People took sides in regard to it and bad feeling was engendered. A council of the church was called to settle the matter, but the bitter feeling was brought into the meeting. Unkind things were said, and these were replied to in like spirit. The excitement grew and in the confusion that followed the opponents of Bro. Bowman succeeded in passing a motion to expel him from the church.

Like numerous others, as we have seen, he refused to accept the verdict of the church as final and refused to count himself out of the church. He went on with his church work preaching, baptizing and officiating at love feasts, as he had done before. Part of the congregation accepted the verdict of the committee and so refused to follow further his leadership. But many went with him, casting their lot with him, and whether he was to be counted in or out of the church, they were willing to accept the same fate.

So far as Bro. Bowman was concerned, however, he seems never to have had any doubt but that he could make reconciliation with the church when he could get to Annual Meeting. But the Civil War was now on, traveling was dangerous and expensive, the Annual Meeting was far away in the north, and so he waited, expecting at the first opportunity, so he had declared to his friends, to go to the Annual Meeting and have the matter adjusted. But alas, this opportunity never came.

Brother Bowman was a man of positive convictions. He was an ardent advocate of peace and thoroughly opposed to war, and his opposition was well known. As war sentiment runs high in times of strife, it is not always prudent to say all that one thinks at such times. This was true in the case of Bro. Bowman. His efforts in the cause of peace had made him enemies in certain circles. In 1863, I think it was, when the war spirit was running high, he was accosted one evening at his home and shot dead by a man in a grey uniform, a true martyr to the cause of religious liberty and freedom of speech.

This left the body of members that he had gathered about him without a leader. They later made application to the General Conference to be restored to the church. A Conference committee was sent to handle the matter. The committee reviewed the case thoroughly and decided that Bro. Bowman had been unjustly expelled. They found no irregularity in his action, and, as regards taking the law, he had done only what the church had granted him permission to do.

Those who had formerly been members of the church were reinstated without confession; and, inasmuch as the expulsion of Bowman was found illegal, the committee decided that all those who had been received into the church after his expulsion should also be received into full fellowship without confession or rebaptism. So the matter was finally adjusted to the satisfaction of all.

The Honites

This body had rather a brief and capricious career. The people were named after their leader, Peter Hon. Peter Hon first came into view among those early immigrants to Kentucky. Here he lived most of his life and seems to have done a good deal of preaching. He was evidently a man of great ability, and swayed his audiences by the power of his eloquence. He was an influential elder and had had an honorable and useful career in the church.

About 1818, or thereabouts, he began to preach strange doctrines. He taught that the communion supper is the Jewish Passover and that the last supper Jesus ate with his disciples was the Jewish Passover. So convincing were his arguments and the power of his eloquence that he led a large number of the Brethren to his way of thinking.

This course of events naturally led to an investigation by the Annual Conference. A committee was sent who went into the case and found that the irregularities with which Peter Hon was charged were true. Since he was unwilling to concede his error and promise to conform his future teaching and action to the established usage of the church, fellowship was withdrawn from him.

Just what effect this action had on the churches in Kentucky is not very clear. But it is certain that many of those who had embraced Hon's doctrines went with him. And this number was so large that it practically broke up the Shelby County church where Hon lived and over which he presided. It is known that the action against Hon included also several other ministers, at least one of whom was an elder. This was in 1820 and was the beginning of the end of the Kentucky churches.

Some years before these events were concluded in Kentucky Hon had begun to visit and preach in Adams County, Ohio. Here he became implicated with the Brethren in southern Ohio. Some of them joined his standard. But for several years his cause did not make much headway. Lately, however, it began to revive. Two young men who had recently been baptized were set apart to the ministry. These now, as if taken by a sudden inspiration, threw themselves soul and body into the cause they had espoused. They created a good deal of excitement; enthusiasm ran high. They had the ability to stir people's emotions and so they held a number of what were regarded as very successful revivals. People were baptized in considerable numbers, and many of these were proselyted from the Brethren. The enthusiasm spread and ran over into the next county.

The cause was prospering. In their success they began to reconstruct some of their teachings. They now repudiated trine immersion and baptized their converts by a single backward action. Things went on in this fashion for several years. A considerable body of members was gathered and much enthusiasm prevailed. These were the real Honites.

But alas, all this was destined to be short lived. These young men had been too successful, they had succeeded beyond what they were able to bear. They became jealous of one another. Each claimed the honor of having built up the work. Then came disparaging statements and covert efforts to diminish each other's influence. Thus jealousy grew into rivalry, rivalry into antagonism, antagonism into open strife.

Of course each had his friends. This divided their congregations into cliques and factions. The excitement with which the members had been gathered was now converted into distraction that drove them apart. And the upshot of the matter was that quarrels, dissensions, strife and rivalry so prevailed among them that, in the absence of any wise leadership or steadying hand, they fell to pieces and disappeared about as suddenly as they had grown up.

It is clear that these two young ministers had never been thoroughly indoctrinated in the principles of the church. This body was more unlike the real spirit and genius of the Brethren, it seems to me, than any other in any way connected with our denominational history.

These two accounts are seen to be in sharp contrast. In the former case the church was at fault for having acted arbitrarily by unjustly expelling a brother. In the second case a cause went to pieces because it was built upon the shifting sands of selfish interest and sentimentality instead of the sure foundation—the grace of God.

CHAPTER VIII

THE CHURCH OF CHRIST AND THE THURMANITES

We have been considering instances of defection or expulsion from the church covering a considerable period of time. We have seen also that these cover generally the territorial extent over which the church had spread. In this chapter we shall consider a few more instances and then turn to other things.

The Church of Christ

The first of the cases that we shall take up in this chapter holds a curious relation to the Brethren; a relationship a little different from any of those we have considered. It is mentioned here more for its curious interest than for its vital relationship to our denominational history.

This story takes us back more than a hundred years to the beginning of the nineteenth century. At that time our people were numerous in the eastern part of Pennsylvania, as they have been ever since. And there were also many other plain people living in close proximity to the Brethren. Among these were Mennonites, Amish and others.

It so happened that two brothers, members of the Mennonite Church, John and Jacob Engle, living in a community of Brethren, became convinced that the

57

Brethren's church practice was in accordance with the teaching of the Bible. So they applied to the Brethren at Germantown to baptize them. After an examination of the applicants, the Brethren refused. There were two reasons for their refusal to baptize the Engles. One was that they did not ask for baptism for the remission of sins, holding that their former baptism by sprinkling had given them absolution from their sins. The other reason was that the Engles did not wish to join the Brethren Church, but they had come to believe that trine immersion was gospel baptism and therefore desired to have it administered. This is how near the River Brethren came to being a part of the Brethren Church.

Although they were refused baptism at the hands of the Brethren, they adopted as their church practice the ordinances almost exactly as the Brethren observed them. About the only exception was that instead of having the supper at the time of communion they ate a common meal before going to church. They lived plain, simple lives, much as the Brethren did, and were often and in many ways identified with them.

The two Engles were active men. They preached their doctrine and gained converts. While they had assumed the title, Church of Christ, they have never been generally known by this name. As they lived along the Susquehanna River, they came to be spoken of as the Brethren by the river and from this as the River Brethren. This name has clung to them and it is the name by which they are generally known.

In theory and practice their faith and manner of life are very similar to the Brethren, and through all their history they have lived on close terms with them. In the migrations of the Brethren from Pennsylvania to other sections west and south, they have frequently gone along as a part of the Brethren colony. In this way they have been scattered to the west and north-west and south. It was by such means that some of them found their way into the Shenandoah Valley in the early part of their history.

They sometimes affiliated with the Brethren and were actually counted as members of the church. An instance of this kind occurred when the Woodstock congregation in Shenandoah County, Virginia, was organized about 1825. There were twelve charter members of this congregation. Six of these were Brethren and six River Brethren. A year after the organization they elected one of their number to the ministry. As it happened this was one of the Brethren. The preaching and services of the church were of course in accordance with the Brethren custom. From this beginning the Woodstock congregation has grown to be one of the well known congregations of the Shenandoah Valley. And, is it strange? or isn't it? When the Progressives withdrew in the eighties the Woodstock congregation suffered most and was the most rent congregation of the Church of the Brethren in Virginia.

The Thurmanites

William C. Thurman was a restless spirit who came

and went among the congregations of the Brethren along in those unsettled years during and after the Civil War. He was a dreamer, an idealist, and was prone to follow vague theories and fancies.

Without pursuing his career in any detail, we will concentrate our attention upon the incident that occurred in Rockingham County, Virginia, where he was a leader among a small group of followers that took his name. He appeared among the churches of the Valley in the summer of 1867. He was a ready talker, an ardent student of the Bible, in his way an interesting and intelligent man; and so he impressed himself favorably upon the Brethren. He was elected to the ministry and soon became an active preacher.

He became especially interested in the subject of the second advent of the Messiah, and by a series of deductions he claimed to have discovered the key to the time element in Christ's second coming. This doctrine he preached with great ardor and convincing power. He soon found himself surrounded by a body of very substantial men and women, loyal and sturdy members of the church who were willing to embrace his doctrine.

He had, by his deductions, worked out as he thought the very day and hour when the Messiah would return. The time set was September 27, 1868, at 10:30 on Sunday morning. One who believed himself in possession of this secret certainly would leave nothing undone to be ready to receive his Lord. It is not remarkable, therefore, that Thurman and his followers took every precaution to be in position to meet the Master, to be caught up into the air with him, and to be forever with the Lord.

Their sincere endeavor to do this no one doubts. But the disappointing details connected with the effort had better be forgotten. It is sufficient for our history to say that Sunday, September 27, 1868, passed by like other Sundays. The calculations had failed of realization.

Gradually the group were disillusioned, and they found themselves in a strange world. But their high standing in character and intelligence made them objects of sympathy rather than of derision. Naturally they repudiated Thurman and cast about for means of adjusting themselves.

They applied for admission into the church again. Those who had formerly belonged were admitted. Those who had been baptized by Thurman and his followers had to be rebaptized. Some of these refused to accept this condition and continued on until the Progressive movement in the early eighties. Then they too were incorporated into that body.

But this had been a harrowing experience and produced very different effects upon those who had been through it. For instance, of four leaders of the church who were drawn into the movement, one came back into the church the most repentant man ever seen; another drifted about, affiliating himself now with this body and now with that, and finally died a Mormon;

the third became a rank infidel; and the fourth lost his mind.

The names of all of these, if they should be mentioned, would sound familiar to persons still living. But to do this would be unkind. So far as this experience goes they are better relegated to the oblivion that is fast gathering about them and this strange illusion.

It is singular what strange things sturdy, intelligent Christians can be induced to believe. It would seem that if anything is clearly taught in the New Testament it is that the time of the second coming of Christ is unknown and unknowable to men. Christ declared that he did not know the time, that the angels of heaven did not know, that nobody knew but the Father. Yet in the face of all this men will presume to know.

God's Word is plain and simple enough for the wayfaring man to understand. But he must read it with an open mind and simple faith, and not with a mind beclouded by prejudice and warped by theories.

CHAPTER IX

THE FREEWILL DUNKERS

Today our flashlight falls upon a scene in the hills of southern Virginia. Here in a genial neighborhood of natural beauty and wholesome rural surroundings, which should have produced a story of true idyllic charm and rustic nobility, was enacted another of those dark histories which cast their lengthening shadows across our story.

It was soon after the close of the Civil War, about 1866 I believe, when John Harvey Lemon moved from Bedford County, Virginia, to Franklin County, same State, and bought a farm a few miles from the old Brick Church which formed the center of a strong community of Brethren. Lemon was an active man, in the first degree of the ministry of the Church of the Brethren, a man of good personality, and had enjoyed educational opportunities above the average of his day. He was a ready speaker, used good language, was intelligent, sociable, a good mixer.

He readily ingratiated himself into the good graces of the neighborhood. He was accounted a good preacher. Members and others liked to hear him. He was orthodox in the interpretation of scripture. He grew steadily into the life of the community. As a farmer, as a neighbor, as a citizen, as a Christian, he was held in high esteem. He was already a man in middle life, probably forty-five years of age.

As time went on he was advanced in the ministry. In the second degree he continued active and was finally ordained to the eldership. He was active in the work of the District and repeatedly served as an official of the District Conference; and on at least one occasion he represented his District on the Standing Committee at Annual Meeting.

It gradually became apparent that he enjoyed popularity. He aspired to be a leader. He began to say unkind things about brethren, especially elders who held positions to which he aspired. Some of the things he said were not true. It became evident that he was seeking to undermine their influence for the purpose of gratifying his own personal ambition. These remarks were the first intimations of any lack of harmony between himself and the church, but other evidence pointing to a lack on his part was soon forthcoming.

He had been in Franklin County some twelve or thirteen years and was farming on a large scale. He had prospered not only in influence but in a material way. He owned several farms and had a number of hired men and women about him. Reports began to be circulated about improper conduct on his part relative to some of his employees. Eye witnesses reported what they had seen and heard, and they were persons whose veracity was not doubted. In fact one was his own son-in-law. But as these witnesses were not members of the Brethren Church their evidence could not be used as conclusive against him. He vigorously denied all the charges made and sternly denounced those who made them.

The charges were, of course, investigated by the Brethren but for lack of usable evidence the case could not be proved and was dropped. As a result of these reports, however, he became inactive in the ministry and seemed to labor under the weight of the accusations. So he disposed of his holdings in Franklin County, selling his farms and personal property, and moved into Floyd County, Virginia. Here he began to preach again and baptized some converts. Now this was just at the time of the Old Order secession in the early eighties. Only a few joined the Old Orders from the southern Virginia churches, but with these few he now cast in his lot and for a time became their leader and minister. Having thus severed himself from the communion of the Brethren, he devoted himself to the propagation of his new cause. But the cause did not develop as he wished and he seemed to grow tired of it. Apparently it did not provide him the opportunity for leadership that he craved.

His next move was to start out for himself. So, organizing the few converts that he had made, he set up his little organization under the banner of Freewill Dunkers. This official designation, however, was seldom used in referring to the sect. They were nearly always called the Lemonites. He seemed to put forth a real effort now to build up his organization. He gave much time and effort to the furtherance of his cause, but with all that he could do, it did not grow.

The field of his former ministerial labors seemed to offer a more inviting prospect. Accordingly he sold out in Floyd County and moved back into Franklin County, some ten or twelve miles from where he had formerly lived. Here he began to preach again on the outskirts of the congregation in which he had faithfully labored for some years. He preached substantially the same doctrines that he had formerly preached, and so began a campaign of proselyting among the members of the church. He won a number of them to his cause. These were chiefly such as lived in somewhat isolated sections, did not get to church very often, and some of them had never been thoroughly indoctrinated into the principles of the church. They represented in the main such as had lacked the best opportunities spiritually, educationally and socially, and, therefore, were less closely united to the church in her deeper interests.

His activity yielded him a considerable congregation. Among the proselytes that he gathered was a young minister, his son-in-law. With this aid in the ministry they bore down with all their weight in an effort to build up their cause but still it grew slowly. At length another effort was made to give it popularity and influence. Lemon joined the masons and became an ardent supporter of the masonic lodge. But he had apparently undertaken the impossible. The doctrines of the Dunkard Church and the ritual of the freemasons would not mix.

Lemon was now growing to be an old man, probably seventy-five years of age. His physical health, which had been strong and robust, began to weaken. Having once begun to give way, he went down rapidly. He sickened and died. The little flock now passed into the hands of his son-in-law. He tried to carry on for a while, but at length seemed to come to the conclusion that it was no use. He moved away into West Virginia and left the flock without a shepherd.

So the movement soon went to pieces. Some of the members came back into the Brethren Church, some went to other churches, and some, seeming to be disgusted with the whole affair, ceased trying to live Christian lives. This was along in the nineties. After a third of a century the ill-considered enterprise is only a memory.

His was a clear case of an inordinate desire for leadership coupled with a lack of moral principle. It was a case in which an ambitious nature was too weak to endure prosperity. With ability and a winning personality, John Harvey Lemon had it in his power to be a useful man in the world and in the church. But the imps of sordidness are ever on the alert. "Whom the gods would destroy they first make mad."

CHAPTER X

THE RISE OF FACTIONS

The middle of the nineteenth century is an epochal date in our history. In general terms, this is the division point between two eras. We have been looking for the most part into local situations. We shall now take a more general view. Looking backward from 1850 we have three-quarters of a century of largely undirected development.

This is a period of migrations. During these years the Brethren Church had spread from the Delaware River to the Rocky Mountains and from Michigan and Iowa to Texas. It was a period of struggle, subduing wild nature, establishing homes and churches. Since the Revolutionary War the church had had no paper and the only means of union among the Brethren was the Annual Meeting, personal letters, and occasional visits.

During this period, there was considerable drifting apart and a consequent difference of usages, as we have seen. But these things were the result of circumstances, and are not to be wondered at.

It is really remarkable that fifty thousand people could have maintained such unity of thought and practice and ideals as existed among the Brethren for three-quarters of a century with such meager external means to unite them. Certainly the Spirit of God had a large place in their thought and life and this kept them largely one.

While there were differences, sometimes serious, as we have seen, there was little of what may be called factions in the church. The differences grew out of local conditions, and even when the Brethren differed, they differed as a rule in fine Christian spirit.

But with the middle of the nineteenth century we enter upon another period of our history. By 1850 the church, which had been almost entirely agricultural, had established itself upon much of the best land of Pennsylvania, Maryland, Virginia, Ohio, and the rich Mississippi and Missouri River basins beyond. Many of the members had prospered, had become well-to-do and lived in ease and plenty. Strong churches had been built up and life had become easier and more leisurely than it once was.

This condition resulted as such conditions usually do. It bred a sort of formalism in the church. The Annual Meeting had through the years grown to be a powerful ecclesiastical body. Its decisions were no longer advisory opinions for the guidance and uniformity of action in the church, but they were beginning to be regarded as statutes that must be obeyed. Meanwhile also the membership of the church generally had come to the condition in life in which they might be assumed to have opinions of their own and the courage and conviction required to express them.

So, at the middle of the nineteenth century, the church was beginning to show evidences of cleavage.

The body was no longer to move forward as a solid phalanx. The movement of the general body was too fast for some and too slow for others. Three groups were soon discernible, and in the quarter of a century following 1850, these three factions came prominently into the limelight.

Factions! yes, that is the word. Smaller bodies within a larger body seeking to dominate it. Not that this was done with any bad motive. On the other hand, I believe that each faction, at least in the early days, was strictly honest in its purposes, and sought power for the sake of making the church what it conceived the church should be.

But still they were factions and worked as factions. One way in which these different interests expressed themselves was in an effort to control the Annual Meeting. The body that could control the Conference would shape the policy of the church. For a quarter of a century the factions struggled earnestly from year to year to gain dominance of this body.

There were now three well defined groups. The great bulk of the membership took a middle course, were conservative and yet forward looking, and stood for the plain principles of the Gospel. Another and much smaller body was eager to go forward much more rapidly than the main body of the church was ready to go. And there was an ultraconservative body that refused to change in any respect from the things that the church had always practiced. All three of these points of view, I believe, were held by their respective adherents with honest conviction and a sincere desire to make the church what they thought it should be.

But the factional spirit was strong and grew stronger year by year. Sharp rivalries developed; a disposition to win, and to defeat the plans of an opponent, was too often apparent. Customs and usages that were profoundly sacred to some Brethren were treated lightly or ridiculed by others; and, it must be admitted, nearly as unwise remarks were sometimes made in rejoinder. " These controversies were carried from the home churches to the District and National Conferences, resulting in bitter personalities, envies, and, it is to be feared, hatred, until, sad to say, Christian affection and brotherly love were strangers in the camp of Israel." One does not need to read far in the church literature of the day to see how intense these rivalries were.

In this same quarter of a century an agency had arisen in our church life that had a great deal to do with the situation just described. This was the church papers. For three-quarters of a century the church had been without a church paper. Now following the middle of the century three separate papers were started by the Brethren in less than twenty years.

Just how these papers related themselves to the factions that developed is not so easy to tell. Whether the factions developed the papers or the papers the factions may be a question. But at any rate they were closely related. Each paper represented the ideas and ideals of a certain group in the Brotherhood. And as was naturally to be expected, as the papers grew in influence and prestige, the lines of cleavage between the different factions became all the more distinctly marked.

As these differences look definitely to further divisions in the church we shall dismiss them for the present and refer briefly yet to the three papers that were so intimately identified with these three groups.

The first of these was the *Gospel Visitor,* first published by Eld. Henry Kurtz in 1851. Bro. Kurtz was a scholarly man, a thorough student of the Bible and a good thinker. He represented the conservative forward looking body of the church. While his adventure met with considerable opposition owing to the fact that a church paper was something new and might cause trouble, and while at the same time queries condemning it were brought to the Annual Conference for a number of years after it began, the editor so skillfully steered clear of any just grounds for criticism that he was eventually given a free hand in his enterprise and opposition ceased.

The second paper was the *Christian Family Companion* which Henry R. Holsinger began to publish at Tyrone, Pennsylvania, in 1864. This weekly was distinctly different in tone from the monthly *Visitor*. The *Companion* advocated various reforms in the church, most of which the church was not yet ready for. Furthermore, it conducted what was known as an open forum in which opportunity was given for

Brethren to express themselves freely in regard to the church and its practices. The opportunity so freely extended was as freely used, and many things were said in the *Companion* that caused deep grief and which had better never been said.

The third of these papers was the *Vindicator* printed at Dayton, Ohio, by Samuel Kinsey in 1870. This at once became the organ of those who believed in the old order of the church, and of course had the effect of confirming those who took this attitude in the position they had assumed and helped to intrench them more deeply in their ultraconservatism.

With the church thus divided in sentiment and each faction supported by a well-established paper advocating its views, it is easy to see what the result is likely to be. But that is another story.

CHAPTER XI

THE OLD GERMAN BAPTISTS

The first of the factions to move toward an independent organization was the Old German Baptists, as they officially styled themselves, but are generally spoken of as the Old Order Brethren. As we have seen, they refused to accept any change in the practice or polity of the church. They were opposed to the publication of the *Gospel Visitor* from the beginning. They were never able to reconcile themselves to some of the teaching that appeared in its columns.

At the Annual Conference of 1857 a rather definite sanction was given to Sunday-schools. Of course, Sunday-schools had been conducted for many years before this at various places by different brethren and sisters but without the sanction of the Conference. The formal granting of leave to carry on Sunday-school work deeply grieved the Old Order Brethren.

But the next year the Conference went on record again in a way that grieved them just as deeply. At this time a query requesting permission to hold evangelistic services, that is, protracted meetings of say a week or two, was cautiously granted by the Conference with advice to be careful and do everything according to the Scriptures and in harmony with the church. At the same meeting was a request for high schools or academies within the church, and the request was not denied.

These facts led to a petition on the part of this element of the church to the Annual Meeting of 1869. They registered their opposition to Sunday-schools, evangelistic meetings, higher education, and now included several other articles. They protested also against prayer meetings and social meetings in the churches. They were still not satisfied with the stand the church had taken on feet washing. They opposed the Annual Meeting's sending committees to local churches to adjust difficulties, holding that this should be the work of adjoining elders. They were also dissatisfied with the way the Standing Committee was selected at the Annual Conference. Instead of selecting the committee from all the elders present from all the States, as was the custom, the Old Order Brethren desired to select six or eight of the oldest elders present from the locality where the Annual Meeting was held.

The Conference considered this petition with due courtesy and framed an answer with a good deal of care. The Conference of course could not grant any of the things the petition had asked for, but it did seek to throw safeguards around all of these innovations that were coming into use. This by no means satisfied the Old Order Brethren but they contented themselves with this reply for a time.

Two years later the matter was again before the Conference and a committee of three elders was appointed to make a thorough study into the ancient practices of the church and bring a report. The committee was D. P. Sayler, Jacob Reiner, and James Quinter. This committee worked on the matter for several years, made a thorough study of the question and carried on an extensive correspondence. They accumulated a considerable quantity of valuable information which they later reported to the Conference.

In anticipation of the findings of this committee, the contentions of the Old Order Brethren were in abeyance for several years. Meanwhile other things occurred that added to their displeasure. As we have seen before, the Far Western Brethren practiced the single mode of feet washing and the Conference of 1859 had declared them in full fellowship with the church, thus sanctioning their practice. The general order of the church, however, except for those Far Western Brethren, had been the double mode. Now in 1877 the Conference authorized the single mode for universal observance. This came as a severe grievance to the Old Order Brethren.

In 1879 many of the elders in the Miami Valley of Ohio, where the Old Order sentiment was exceptionally strong, met together and framed a series of grievances which they presented in the form of a petition to the Conference of 1880. They repeated most of the things mentioned in their former petition —Sunday-schools, academies, protracted meetings, the mode of feet washing—and added their protest against a salaried ministry, or ministers receiving pay for ministerial service.

This petition was respectfully considered by the Conference. But as it was impossible to grant any of the requests, the safeguards urged by the Conference report only agitated the question, because the Conference had actually given its assent to these practices.

It was clearly evident to the Old Order Brethren now that they could not control the Annual Conference, and the only way in which they could carry out their views would be to organize themselves into an independent body. They determined, however, to make one more petition to the Conference of 1881. This they did but received no comfort or consolation, yet being treated with all possible courtesy and consideration. They withdrew and a short time after effected an organization of their own.

They organized under the name Old German Baptist Brethren. At first they were by no means a homogeneous body but represented those who were opposed to the various changes that had been taking place in the church. Some were opposed to one innovation, some to another. Probably those who were opposed to all the various changes that had taken place in the church were very few, but their defection from one cause or another brought them all into one body.

How many left the church in this movement has never been definitely ascertained, but the number was probably in the neighborhood of four thousand. In some sections, as in Ohio and Indiana, considerable congregations were at once organized. But in many places they left in very small bodies or as individuals, many of whom were after this without a church home.

They held their first Annual Meeting in 1882 on Whitsuntide at Brookville, Ohio, and it is said that they had representatives present from nine States of

the union. They have continued to hold their Annual
Conferences at this season, and I am told, to the present day hold their meetings, as the Brethren once did,
with a love feast in connection and feeding large numbers of people free of charge.

Through the years since their organization they have
gradually dwindled in numbers. They have not been
able to attract those from the outside, neither have they
been able to hold their own children. They continue
their opposition to higher education, Sunday-schools,
prayer meetings, evangelistic services, foreign and
home mission work and all other organized charities
and philanthropies.

They are without a program of church work, live
for themselves and their families, have no outlook upon
the world and seem to feel no responsibility for it.
This is not true because they are niggardly or miserly
or wanting in generosity. No one could be more hos-
pitable than they are in their homes. Their public
and private lives are above reproach. Their simple
worship is reverent and devout. They represent some
of the finest domestic virtues to be found anywhere.

What a pity that so much goodness of heart and
sincerity of purpose and tender sympathy and benevo-
lence, all of which this troubled world needs so much,
should go unused and unfelt! But without a feeling
of responsibility for others, without a program for
religious work, without an outlook, or sense of personal stewardship, there can be but one result. A lack
of vision can mean only darkness, and where there is
no vision the people perish.

CHAPTER XII

THE BRETHREN CHURCH

After the Old Order Brethren had taken their departure and launched out for themselves, it was only a short time until the so-called Progressive element made a similar move. The two cases were not parallel however. The Old Order Brethren left the church. They withdrew because the church would not keep house according to their ideas.

In the case of the Progressives, they organized after one of their leaders had been expelled from the church. This was Henry R. Holsinger, of Pennsylvania. For a good many years Bro. Holsinger had been at variance with the church. He held views almost diametrically opposite to those held by the Old Order Brethren, and in some respects radically different from those generally held by the church.

We have seen that his free rostrum in the *Christian Family Companion* was constantly widening the difference between himself and the church at large. He was repeatedly called to account by the Annual Conference for disparaging statements about the church which he had made or sanctioned, and although these matters were patched up for the time being, new offenses kept up the disturbance and dissatisfaction.

After running his paper nearly nine years, he sold it to Eld. James Quinter in 1873. While the editorial policy of the paper was not changed under its new management the tone was considerably different. The free rostrum was continued, but the tone was not offensive and the editorial policy was constructive and conciliatory.

It is not possible to go into much detail in this history, and we should be careful not to accuse Henry R. Holsinger unjustly. There is no doubt that the church needed changes in the various lines that he advocated, but his method of bringing them about was not calculated to produce the desired end. He did not have the tact or skill required for leadership in such an enterprise. I would not for a moment impeach his good motives in what he was trying to do. But his ardent nature, his impetuous temperament, too often led him to make rash and unguarded statements which hurt his cause more than they helped it.

In the fall of 1878 he again launched into an editorial enterprise. In company with J. W. Beer he began printing at Berlin, Pennsylvania, a weekly paper called the *Progressive Christian*. The paper assumed a radical policy and became actually abusive in its denunciation of many usages of the church and those who believed in them. After running less than two years the paper failed.

If the *Christian Family Companion* had given offense by its open forum, the *Progressive Christian* was a worse offender. If the editor of the *Companion* had been free spoken, the editor of the *Progressive Christian* was more so. If many Brethren had been grieved by the *Companion,* they were not only grieved but mortified by the *Progressive Christian.* It was evident by this procedure that the extreme liberal faction of the church was leading to a crisis.

Of course petitions to the Annual Meeting of 1879 protesting against Holsinger and his paper were numerous. Protests came from at least half a dozen State Districts in Ohio, Pennsylvania, Maryland and Virginia, representing the sections in which the church was strongest and most representative.

A good deal of time was taken at the Conference dealing with the matter. It was at length patched up, promises were made, and probably some went away with hopes that things might be better.

A year later the *Progressive Christian* was revived, and at the Conference at Ashland, Ohio, in 1881, protests against the paper and its editor were again numerous. This time they came chiefly from the middle west, from Illinois, Indiana, Ohio, and Missouri. Two whole days of the Conference were taken up in considering these complaints. These deliberations closed with the appointment of a committee of five elders who were to go to Berlin, Pennsylvania, try the case, and deal with the offender according to his transgression.

In the stormy trial which occupied two days the factious spirit was in full evidence. The patience of the committee was sorely tried, things were said and done that had better been left unsaid and undone. In the end, however, they framed a report which they presented to the congregation. The congregation refused to accept the report, and the committee departed leaving the whole matter in a very unsettled condition.

The Berlin report, as it was called, was presented to the Annual Conference of the next year (1882). A good deal of time was taken in considering it. Many of the leading elders and ministers of the Brotherhood were present and took part in the discussion. Opportunity was given for a thorough ventilation of the matter. The report found H. R. Holsinger guilty of insubordination and an unwillingness to hear the church. It therefore recommended withdrawal of membership from him. Thus the acceptance of the report meant the expulsion of Holsinger. When the report was finally placed upon its passage, it was approved by an almost unanimous vote.

Steps were immediately taken by Holsinger and his friends to form a temporary organization. Of course he had many sympathizers and a considerable number of these were at the Conference. They met the next day at a schoolhouse a mile from the Conference grounds and among other things decided to meet at Ashland, Ohio, on the 29th of June in order to determine more definitely their future procedure.

They effected an organization, calling themselves the Progressive Brethren Church, and extended cordial invitations to all who were aggrieved in the churches to join them. They adopted a declaration of principles and prepared for a vigorous campaign of evangelism and proselyting.

During the year that followed there was much activity in the Progressive camp. They were active in effecting organizations of members wherever opportunity afforded and evangelistic efforts were planned for the most strategic points. Much of the preaching was characterized by strong denunciation and sometimes downright abuse, but this was not always confined to one side. There was also considerable wrangling over church property and legal procedures were resorted to.

Overtures were made to the Conference of 1883, but the Conference found no cause to reconsider its former action. Shortly after this Conference a meeting was held at Dayton, Ohio, at which the Progressives and two other bodies that had gone off from the Brethren —the Congregationals and the Leedy Brethren—were organized into a new denomination under the name of the Brethren Church.

The defection of the Progressives marks the largest body that has ever pulled off from the Brethren. How many there were at first there is no way of knowing, but as a group they were somewhat larger than the Old Order group. The church published no statistics until 1895, when they had been an independent body for thirteen years. In the meantime they had been actively engaged in building up their membership and had associated with themselves at least three other bodies entire. In their Annual Conference of 1895 they reported a total membership of 10,031 members.

The Brethren Church has been an active, energetic

body. They hold in the main the doctrines of the Church of the Brethren, although they have practically neglected some of the doctrines that the mother church always held and still holds dear; such for instance as the simple life and opposition to secret, oath-bound societies.

While earnest and active, they are a small body to carry on an effective church program. They have one college, missions in Africa and South America, and are endeavoring to supply their congregations with pastors. But even a reasonable support of these enterprises is beyond their financial resources. While they have grown in some sections in a commendable way, in other sections they have closed churches, often leaving a small body of members without ministerial aid or other means of spiritual nurture.

All the things for which they left the church are now maintained by the mother church. If they could only have had the patience to wait a little, their ideals would have been much more fully realized than they have been by withdrawal.

It is fair to say that there were others in the church in the early eighties who were as progressive as Holsinger and his followers and who saw the needs of the church as clearly as did they. But they did not wish to go faster than they could carry the body of the church with them. So this disruption came as a result of radical leadership, an impatient spirit, and a lack of deliberation and self-control. It could and should have been avoided.

CHAPTER XIII

THE DUNKARD BRETHREN

It would seem that we have made enough mistakes of one kind—that of pulling apart and separating from one another—but we will have to record at least one other instance.

After the lopping off of the two extremes in the early eighties, the church enjoyed its greatest period of progress and prosperity. There has been a unanimity of sentiment and a oneness of aim and effort that had not characterized our denominational life for many years before.

During this period also, the church grew as it had never before grown. After the divisions in the eighties, carefully compiled statistics revealed our church population to be about fifty-eight thousand. It took us more than a hundred and sixty years to grow to that membership. Today we number at least a hundred and thirty thousand, having more than doubled our membership in less than fifty years.

In this half century or less the church has wonderfully expanded its activities. It has established and developed vigorous missions in the three great sections of the heathen world—India, China and Africa. It has built up a series of Christian colleges which, in ideals and standards of work, rank with the best in the land. It has taken a leading place in the development of Sunday-school work and, by building new churchhouses and adapting old ones, is providing up-to-date facilities for religious teaching. It has developed an efficient system of charities to take care of its aged poor and orphan children. It has built up a fine work among the women of the church through the Aid Societies and otherwise. It fosters the spiritual development of the young through a well organized and efficiently administered Y. P. D. in the different grades. It is gradually developing a system of providing pastoral care of the churches. It is providing a body of well prepared and carefully edited church literature of high grade. In its various activities, the church evinces a grasp of its work and a vision of its mission that should be gratifying to all who have the interests of the Kingdom at heart.

Notwithstanding all this, in the recent years there have appeared signs of restlessness in certain quarters. This has been due to a small body of members here and there who insist on looking backward instead of forward. They are ready to raise a question about anything that is done in a different manner from what it was formerly done.

To them the church is a fixed institution. It can not change. It must work like it used to work, it must look like it used to look. They forget that the church is to serve the world. Although the world is constantly changing, the church must continue to do its work as it did in the " good old times " of long ago. When the church adapts its methods of work to meet changed conditions, they raise the cry of apostasy, departure from the faith. So they become dissatisfied and fail to coöperate with the body.

For the last dozen years or more this dissatisfaction has been in evidence. Queries or petitions were several times brought to the general Conferences designed to " bring back " the church to its former ways of doing things. While these papers received courteous treatment at the hands of the Conference, the requests, because of their reactionary character, could not be granted. Failing to receive Conference support of their contentions, the agitators sought to advance their cause by other means.

About 1923 B. E. Kesler and others began to publish a paper at Poplar Bluff, Missouri, in which they gave expression to this dissatisfaction. The paper was entitled, *Bible Monitor,* and appeared monthly. Later it was changed to a semi-monthly. This naturally became the rallying point for those of kindred feeling. In magnifying the differences between themselves and the church and in fomenting harsh feelings the paper probably served its purpose. It became an agency to crystallize the discontent into fixed opposition, which seemed to regard itself as irreconcilable with the church.

Accordingly steps were taken to withdraw from the church and organize an independent body. This was done in June, 1926, at Plevna, Indiana. An organization was effected under the title, Dunkard Brethren, which has since been incorporated. A year later, June, 1927, at a conference near Goshen, Indiana, a form of doctrine and practice and a system of church polity were formally adopted. This done, the appointment of certain boards and committees completed the work of the organization.

This whole matter resembles so much another of which I have read that the comparison is inevitable. A certain man found himself at odds with those about him, so he went off and set up for himself. When his brethren and all his father's house heard it they went down thither to him. And every one that was in distress, and every one that was in debt, and every one that was discontented for any cause, gathered themselves unto him; and there were in all about four hundred men.

I would not misrepresent the Dunkard Brethren, I would not question their motives. So far as I know they are good meaning men and women, but they are sadly mistaken. The idea that a little band of elderly people, dissatisfied with local conditions in the church, some for one thing and some for another, widely scattered, can organize themselves into a working body that can get anywhere, and that on a reactionary program, is unthinkable.

It is sometimes the case that those who can not get along with the church can not get along with one another; and there are evidences that this is true in this case. We hear of differences already in a little group of eleven that went off at one place less than a year ago. And one of these has already seen the error of his way and has been restored. We are glad to learn that in other places some have returned to the mother church.

At a meeting in which an effort was made to get members to " sign up," some one raised the question as to why they should leave the church. It was answered, " To get away from the worldliness in the church." Pressed for specific instances of worldliness, " Life insurance, a hireling ministry, neckties, musical instruments in worship," were among the forms of worldliness named. A little quick thinking and observation revealed the fact that about all these things were already represented among those who had " signed up." No wonder the meeting broke up in confusion.

The tendency to worldliness is an ever present evil and in the church life of our time, as in the days of the apostles and in every age since, we find things that grieve the hearts of the faithful. The trend toward carnality and materialism is strong. We must continue to labor diligently for greater consecration, " for an increase of holiness in ourselves and others." But the idea of a new and separate Dunkard Brethren church is a mistake. These good people have nothing to offer the world that the church from which they withdrew does not have.

CHAPTER XIV

SOME REFLECTIONS

Of those who have followed these flashlights, I wonder how many are proud of the history they reveal. How many think better of themselves and the church turbed over details that have been magnified out of all proportion to their importance, and in our anxiety because these things were done? How have they one another. We have allowed ourselves to be dis- about these things we have sometimes forgotten the denominational history? Yet a whole chapter of our enriched our church life or reflected credit upon our church record has been taken up with just these things. We have taken to ourselves a very endearing name: developed a remarkable ability to get on agreeably with we insist on being called Brethren. Yet we have not

We have always been a pious and modest people. finer things of our Christian profession.

As we look back over these experiences from longer range, all of us no doubt regret that so much time and effort, that might have been much more helpfully employed, were spent in these ways. Our distance in time from most of these experiences has softened the tints in which they were beheld and has taken away the sharp edge of the annoyance that in their time was so grievous. But to the Brethren of those days these grievances were very real and very important.

Is it not singular that people of the gentle spirit that has always characterized the Brethren should allow themselves to be so wrought upon that congregations should be divided, members disfellowshiped by the dozens if not by the hundreds, the church rent and mangled, the lives of well meaning Brethren embittered, and even some of them sent to their graves in disappointment and sorrow?

And what was it all about? At one time it was feet washing, the symbol of humility, fellowship and service. Not that there was any question about the validity of the rite, or the importance of it, or whether it should be celebrated as an ordinance of the church. These things were never in question. But the matter that shook the church to its foundation was as to *how the ordinance should be administered.*

At another time the trouble was mysticism, a failure to see clearly the plain simple teachings of the Gospel, and going off after fads and frills and fancies. Of course, this involved a comparatively small body of members, but in the infant days of the church the movement made disastrous inroads on the church.

At another time it was intolerance, allowing personal feeling rather than the spirit of Christian forbearance to rule in the administration of church affairs. At another time it was the second coming of Christ. Although Jesus had clearly stated that he did not know when his second advent should take place, yet men presumed to know. At another time it was mere impatience, and at other times things as trivial and unimportant.

So it was when the Brethren lost themselves in theories, in speculations, in misguided emotions, in arbitrary action, they went wrong. As we look back to these divisions in the church, usually caused by a small group of members losing their bearings and thus coming in conflict with the body of the church, it is evident that all these separations were mistakes. Of all that have been discussed, and no effort was made to be exhaustive, there was not one but should have been avoided. The disputes over these things and the actions that followed were all negative, they helped nobody, they helped no cause; but they weakened the church, they discouraged members and sometimes blasted lives.

We would be far from saying there was no cause for these misunderstandings and differences. The church is made up of human beings and humanity is never infallible. There were no doubt things that should have been remedied, but the method used to find the remedy was in every case a mistake. Amputating a limb should be the last desperate remedy to save a life; so disrupting churches and breaking up homes should be the last expedient in church work.

Sad as these experiences were, they reveal one thing that is comforting. These eruptions were never deep-seated. They did not have to do primarily with articles of faith, or seriously question the doctrines of the church. They were superficial in their nature—mere excrescences, eruptions on the surface, boils and pimples and blotches that healed in time without deeply affecting the entire body.

There is no doubt that the Brethren did not distinguish clearly between the doctrines of the church and the methods to be employed in carrying them into practice. But it is perfectly clear now that no principle of Christian faith was ever vitally at stake and that the contentions were simply over methods of administration.

So despite all these disturbances on the surface, the deep down life of the church has always been sound. And in this the Church of the Brethren has been peculiarly blessed. While many other Christian bodies have been rent and shaken by internal dissension, I am disposed to think that the heart life of our general church body has never been deeply affected. We have magnified details of administration until they loomed with ominous terror, but we did this because we did not see clearly their relative significance. We erred in judgment and lack of vision. The faith of the church was not impaired and its heart was sound and true.

It is to be hoped we have learned the lesson these experiences teach. Division hasn't helped the church or those that have gone off from it. Neither has it redounded to the church's credit either intellectually or spiritually. Members have found it too easy to be at variance with one another, often about trivial and unimportant matters. While tithing mint and rue and cummin, we have sometimes neglected the weightier matters of the law.

PART II

FORCES THAT UNIFY

CHAPTER XV

THE COLONIAL CHURCH

I wish I were an artist, I would like to paint a picture; not on canvas with pencil and brush, but with words. My picture would not be a portrait but the aggregate of numerous portraits. It would be a picture of society, of a particular society, in a definite time and place. The picture would be that of a religious society, the community life of the church I love—The Church of the Brethren.

The scene of this picture would be Eastern Pennsylvania, and the picture would seek to delineate the life there from the time Peter Becker with his little body of German exiles landed at Philadelphia to the time of the Revolutionary War. This is a period of a little more than a half century and it is one unique in our denominational life.

Are you able to visualize the church of that time? Are you able to see those godly men and women as they actually lived their lives in that day? Can you go with them into their homes, see them around their hearthstones, hear the earnest yearnings of their hearts as they poured them out around the family altar?

Can you go with them into their shops and factories and other places of business and see them buy and sell and trade with their neighbors? Can you understand the type of dealing they carry into their business relations? Can you go with them into their places of worship? Can you see them around the congregational altar? Can you catch the spirit of their sermons, their prayers, their teaching? Can you feel the spirit of that earnest life that emanated from them in all their relations with one another and with others?

This is a picture I would like to paint. Let us see if we can divest ourselves of other things so that we can see it together.

I have referred to the church of this time as a small body, and it was. During these first fifty years of the church in this country the total membership at no time probably exceeded a thousand souls. And I have wondered sometimes whether any other thousand men and women anywhere ever made a profounder impression upon their time than did the little Church of the Brethren before the Revolutionary War.

These were years of beginnings, years when lines of church polity had to be worked out, when the commands of the Gospel had to be adapted to the needs of society, when the church as an organization had to shape itself into an institution to meet the world's needs.

It may not be easy to understand what this signifies. This church had once before offered its services of comfort and help to a needy people, but found it impossible to exist in the society from which it emerged. Harassed and persecuted and driven from place to place, these children of God would probably have found it impossible to persist in their efforts to worship him according to the dictates of their conscience in the old world, and so the cause would have failed had not Providence made possible the escape to the new. Now for a second time this little body of believers is offering the grace which it has found so precious to a new society under a new environment.

Let us see what this little body stood for. What kind of institution had it evolved? What kind of a church organization did it invite its neighbors and friends into? It was one in every way creditable to their lofty conception of character and their ideals of the true mission of Jesus Christ.

To begin with, their congregations were presided over by bishops who were not only ecclesiastical dignitaries but were true shepherds of the flock. They gave to their congregations an oversight and spiritual leadership that the church has never surpassed, if it has equalled, to this day. A system of salaried pastors was as yet unknown, but without recompense or even a thought of it, these early leaders made the care of their charges their first consideration. Under their system of voluntary pastorates they developed in their membership a high type of spirituality and a general nobility of character that has seldom been equalled. Christianity in that society was more than a name, more than a profession—it was a life.

These godly leaders introduced into their church life various agencies as aids in the attainment of their ideals. A generation before the modern Sunday-school was even thought of, the Brethren had provided a system of teaching by which the young people could receive religious instruction at the hands of the church. The Brethren were the real founders of the modern Sunday-school enterprise. They provided suitable care for the poor of the church and set a glowing example of Christian responsibility and liberality to the Christendom of their day. They fostered education, were active in the promotion of not only elementary education, but they also fostered institutions of higher rank. They believed in organized charities and made liberal contributions to the same. They encouraged intelligence in all phases of life and were active in the production and dissemination of literature in its various forms. They built up and conducted one of the most enterprising printing establishments in the colonies. Through the press and otherwise their leaders boldly raised their voices against evils of every sort. They stood staunchly for the purity and integrity of the home and were always found on the side of morality, justice, uprightness, freedom, purity, and righteousness.

Let us look in a little detail at some of the matters of public concern in which they interested themselves.

To begin with, the Brethren Church was the first antislavery society in this country. When William Lloyd Garrison started his *Liberator* in 1831 the country was thoroughly entrenched in slavery. The constitution of the United States guaranteed it, the supreme court upheld it, and there was little feeling of public conscience against it; and this had been true through all the history of the colonies and the nation.

During all of this apathy, however, of the American people to the traffic in human souls the Brethren Church was with one or two exceptions the only organization in the land that raised its voice of protest against the nefarious institution. Fifty years before Garrison began his agitation, the Brethren Church had written into the records of her Annual Conference this declaration: " It has been unanimously considered that it cannot be permitted in any wise by the church that a member should or could purchase negroes and keep them as slaves." This was enacted at the Annual Meeting of 1782.

But even twenty-three years before this, in 1759, one of the leading members of the church wrote a book against slavery in which he denounced the institution as godless, wicked, and inconsistent with the profession of the followers of Christ. So it was, that long before there was any public conscience in regard to human slavery in this country, the Church of the Brethren had taken a position of absolute opposition to the traffic in the souls of men.

Substantially the same thing was true in regard to temperance. About the first organized opposition to intemperance in this country was the formation of the Washingtonian Society in 1840. John B. Gough, an Englishman, took the temperance pledge in 1842 and almost immediately thereafter began his career of lecturing against the evil, the cause to which he gave the rest of his life. This was the beginning of temperance agitation.

Neal Dow of Maine is generally accredited, however, with being the father of the prohibition movement in this country. In 1851 he was instrumental in having the first state law passed against the drink evil. This Maine law has been the model and forerunner of the modern crusade against intemperance. It was in this same year, 1851, that a temperance society known as the Good Templars was organized. Eighteen years later, in 1869, the prohibition party had its origin out of this organization. This party has been largely instrumental in keeping the cause of temperance before the country from that day to this.

In 1874, the women of the country organized themselves to combat this evil. The Woman's Christian Temperance Union was organized in this year at Cleveland, Ohio, with Frances E. Willard as secretary. Five years later Miss Willard became president of the organization, to the promotion of which she gave the rest of her life, and left the organization with five hundred thousand women enlisted in the cause.

Notwithstanding all this splendid activity in a great moral crusade within the last hundred years, the Brethren Church espoused the cause of temperance a hundred years before there was any organized opposition against it in this country. As early as 1741 the Brethren were lecturing against intemperance, publishing articles and tracts and books against it, and raised their voices fearlessly in opposition to the terrible social scourge, in a time when there was practically no sentiment against it. And in 1783, fifty-seven years before the Washingtonian Society was organized, the

Brethren wrote into the minutes of their Annual Conference a decision to withdraw Christian fellowship from all members who refused to put away their distilleries.

Here was another pioneer record against a great social wrong. It was not enough simply to abstain from the use of intoxicants, but to distil liquor and dispense it to others was, in the estimation of the early church, so inconsistent with the Christian profession that persons who insisted on so doing could not be held as members in the Church of the Brethren.

As regards the principle of peace, the Brethren likewise put themselves on record. They, along with the Quakers, the Mennonites, and possibly one or two other small bodies were almost the only people in the country to raise their voices against war until our own day. In fact it took the enormity of the World War to bring home to the hearts of Christendom the fact that war is sin and is inconsistent with the teachings of Jesus Christ. But this doctrine the Brethren held and firmly advocated for more than a hundred and fifty years before the World War. As early as 1748 the Brethren were writing books and pamphlets against the terrible institution.

If it is objected that during these years, although the church was advocating these doctrines it was not actually engaged in promoting them, the answer simply is that no one can tell how much they have contributed to the enlightenment of the world on these great moral issues, by consistently upholding and advocating them, both in theory and practice, and thus making themselves examples in a great humanitarian cause before the world. It is my firm conviction that they deserve unqualified praise for their adherence to great moral principles through terrible devastating wars in which they have stood out in heroic boldness and fidelity for principles to which the Christian world of our day is giving its unanimous approval.

There are other great causes also to which the Brethren Church has priority of claim. One of these is the promotion of Sunday-school work. The first Sunday-school of modern times was held in a Brethren Church, in Germantown, Pennsylvania. More than forty years before Robert Raikes began his Sunday-school work in Gloucester, England, the Brethren at Germantown conducted a school on Sunday afternoon adapted especially to the interests of the young people.

They were also among the first, if not the very first people in this country, to provide homes for the old folks and orphans of the church. Institutions of this kind in our day are everywhere, and are fostered by churches, States, philanthropic societies, public spirited citizens, and in many other ways. But a hundred and seventy years ago it was not so. There were then no provisions for the care of the unfortunate and homeless. As early as 1760 the Brethren had set aside a building which they furnished and provided rent free to the poor widows of the church. This was the beginning of the old folks' home idea in this country.

These are some of the principles for which the

early church stood. Let them suffice to indicate the spirit of the Church of the Brethren in colonial times. Let us see now if we can catch the manner of life of these early Brethren.

These men were practical exemplars of an everyday type of Christianity. Carrying their religion into the affairs of daily living, they set a standard of conduct that has seldom been equalled. When good business management had made a business venture of one of them especially profitable, we see him doubling his return to his patrons without increase of cost to them and justifying his course by protesting that " one must not allow himself to be paid double." When the proprietor of the famous publishing house at Germantown found himself growing rich from the prosperity of his business, he printed a religious magazine, the first of its kind in America, and distributed the copies generously and free of cost to those that received them. And this he did to the extent of sixty-four issues, many of them double numbers, and covering a period of eight years.

Here is a standard of Christian living in which the practice is no whit behind the profession.

An unscrupulous man once undertook to take the advantage of the second Christopher Sower because of his principle of nonresistance. He owed Sower a sum of money and vowed he would not pay it unless Sower compelled him to do so by process of law. The good man refused to use the law and the other stoutly maintained his refusal to pay. Sower at length cancelled the debt and destroyed the note. When he had almost forgotten the matter the man came into his office one day in a state of great agitation. He had the money all counted out in full payment of principal and interest to the very day.

" I have come to pay you what I owe you," said the man.

" You do not owe me anything," Sower replied.

" Yes I do," was the hasty retort, " and I want you to take it. I cannot rest until it is paid."

" But I have no right to the money," continued Sower, " I destroyed the note and closed the account."

" No matter, I must pay the bill," he went on. " I can have no peace of mind until it is settled. Tell me what I can do."

Elder Sower named a charitable institution to which a donation would be welcome and highly beneficial. The man turned over the full sum and in doing so eased his conscience, let us hope, at the same time that he discharged an honest debt.

In addition to these remarkable instances of noble living what personalities these men developed! What manly men, what womanly women! How they ranked with the noblest, the greatest, the best of their day! With what a dignity they invested their church, their enterprises, the institutions through which they touched life at its various points! We have had nothing like it since. Our leaders of that day are among the great men of colonial America. In learning, in culture, in character, in ability, in manliness in all those fine virtues that make for goodness and greatness, our early leaders were second to none. They were powerful because they were godly. They made righteous living the chief purpose of their existence.

At the same time that Benjamin Franklin was laying the foundation for an academy in Philadelphia, which later developed into the University of Pennsylvania, Christopher Sower as president of the trustees of the Germantown Academy was laying the foundation for liberal education in Germantown. At the same time that Franklin was building up his printing business on the banks of the Delaware, the first Christopher Sower was building a similar institution eight miles away on the banks of the Schuylkill.

It is not strange that these two men of big business in their day, in a sense rivals, should sometimes clash in their business interests, and they did, and this more than once. But in each instance Sower acquitted himself in a manner that gave even the wily, discreet Franklin no advantage over him. And when it comes to integrity of character, nobility of ideals, the rock bottom foundation of Christian deportment, Sower showed an elevation of spirit and a regard for principles of right and honor that even overshadowed those of his great rival.

So the colonial Church of the Brethren numbered in its membership some of the greatest men of that day. In the two Christopher Sowers it had two of the leading business men and publishers of the country.

In the Drexels it had among the ablest financiers in the colonies. In the first Alexander Mack it had an unwavering leader of clear vision scarcely equalled elsewhere. In John Naas it had an example of Christian tolerance that put the practice of the New England Puritans to shame. In Peter Becker it manifested a spirit of fervent devotion and deep spirituality seldom surpassed. In the second Alexander Mack it produced one of the greatest poets of colonial America. It produced the first religious magazine in the new world. It published the Bible first translated into a European language. And what more can I say?—this infant church led the world of its day in Christian teaching, in bringing systematic religious instruction to the young through agencies provided by the church. This infant church disseminated useful information through the agency of the printing press to the isolated sections of colonial America, where it brought comfort, instruction, advice, help to needy homes. Yes, it set a standard for piety, honesty and nobility of life, that has not been surpassed, if it has been equalled, anywhere else. I am proud to be a member of a church that has produced men and women like these.

CHAPTER XVI

THE CHURCH UNDER TRIAL

This is to be a picture set in a black frame and draped in mourning. It is a picture of a society discouraged, heartbroken, downcast and sorrowing—our little mother church with its high idealism, its spirit of helpfulness, its shining example of altruism and self-sacrifice, caught in the whirl of a relentless war and all but ground to death between the upper and nether millstone—in short, a picture of the church at the time of the Revolutionary War and the years immediately following.

To understand what this picture means we will have to go back a little. We will need to understand the conditions in Pennsylvania before the war came on. We usually think of early Pennsylvania history in terms of William Penn and the Quakers. But the Quakers were by no means the only people to make the Keystone State their home. Probably no one of the colonies at the beginning of the Revolution had a more heterogeneous population than did Pennsylvania. Out of this condition grew at least some of the elements that give color to our picture.

It is estimated that at the outbreak of the Revolution Penn's colony numbered about three hundred thousand souls, and these were almost equally divided into three groups. There were the English Quakers, the first inhabitants of the colony. Then there was about an equal number of Germans representing many sects, and these for the most part of the sternly Protestant type such as the Mennonites, the Amish, the Moravians, the Brethren. The third group were English loyalists of the worldly cavalier class who, for the most part, became patriots in the war.

It is readily understood that the first two of these groups were lovers of peace and opponents of war of every kind; and they constituted two thirds of the population. The Germans, because of prejudice against them, had never figured largely in the public life of the colony; and by the time of our story, under stress of the aggression from the British government in recent years, the Quakers had also fallen into disfavor, so that the government of the colony had passed into the hands of the third group. These assumed the rôle of patriots and would have had it understood that they were the only patriots in the colony. In fact, the Quakers and many of the Germans were branded as Tories and therefore disloyal.

It was out of these conditions that the little Church of the Brethren was called upon a second time to wring its heart in blood in order to maintain its physical existence and live the principles it had espoused. Under the stress of war the colonial government passed a measure aimed directly at the pacifists of all shades in the province. The law required every citizen of the colony to subscribe to an oath renouncing allegiance to the British government and pledging allegiance to the colony of Pennsylvania. The government of the colony was pledged to unyielding prosecution of the war against England and every loyal citizen must devote himself unreservedly to this policy. This of course the Brethren could not do.

It requires no stretch of imagination to see the effects of this state of things upon the church, and it should be recorded as a monument to the unwavering Christian integrity of the Brethren that with rare exceptions they stood true to their allegiance to Christ and his principles of peace regardless of what might happen to them personally.

One of two things usually happened. Many of them resorted to the expedient that a former generation of their ancestors had used: they fled from the persecution. The war started great tides of emigration—westward and southward. Among the emigrants were many of the Brethren. They preferred to leave their homes, often abandoning everything they could not carry with them, almost without compensation, preferring to start life anew elsewhere rather than endure the persecutions and hardships under which they lived. It was under conditions like these that the famous Wolfe family moved west and later south into Kentucky and still later into the then far west. It was at this time that the Saylers and Bixlers and others escaped into Maryland. The same conditions brought the Garbers, the Wines, the Myerses, and many others into Virginia.

These emigrations naturally weakened the churches of Pennsylvania, taking away frequently some of the leading and most enterprising spirits. Those who left went off into new countries and lost themselves for the time being in their efforts to establish new homes and wring a subsistence from a wild and exacting world. Those who remained were subjected to many discouragements and persecutions, and were harassed often by the loss of their property and the unjust scorn and contempt that is heaped upon the adherents of an unpopular cause. All this was hard on the little Church of the Brethren.

We must now dismiss for the present these who remain at home and allow them to bear their persecutions as best they may, while we follow the emigrants, in imagination, to their new homes. Can you see them loading their wives and children and household furniture into their wagons, abandoning some of the heavy and bulky articles because they cannot be taken along, bidding adieu to the humble cottage which had been to them home, driving off with what the horses can haul, leading a few cows and colts behind the wagon, and the little family moving slowly off into the distance to be lost in the wilderness and forests of an almost uninhabited world?

Multiply this incident over and over and over again and see these lumbering wagons plodding on day after day, week after week, through almost uninhabited and roadless regions until they finally reach a place which seems to afford them opportunity to make a living and worship God according to the dictates of their conscience. Here they make a halt, purchase a tract of land for a few dollars an acre, for which they mortgage the farm and their personal property. Then with their own hands they fell the trees and build a log cabin in the forest and start life anew. With the forests and wild beasts and wild Indians to deal with these men and women go resolutely about building themselves new homes, rearing their families, worshiping God, but cut off from the rest of the world, unknown and unheard of outside of the community into which they have gone. But this they endured, and did it willingly, for the sake of their faith in the Christ whom they served.

In this way the faith of the Brethren was carried in a few years to many new and remote sections— to western Pennsylvania and Ohio; southward into Maryland, Virginia, Tennessee and Kentucky; and for the time at least, most of these places had no communication with others. The church had literally buried itself in the forests and on the prairies of the new world. Here we must leave them for the present. You may picture them by the power of imgination in their struggles to establish themselves in their new environment.

But we must come back and see what is going on among those who did not leave. While those who sought new homes in distant sections had their hardships and their trials, those who remained had their difficulties of another kind. During the war they were subjected to many barbarities. They were robbed, lied about, calumniated, ridiculed, hated and, it is said, sometimes killed. But they were willing to bear it all rather than compromise their allegiance to their Lord and Master.

Let me make the picture concrete by citing a few instances. Christopher Sower the second, at the time of the Revolution, was at the height of his prosperity and influence. His uncompromising opposition to war made him a conspicuous target for his enemies. This was all the more true because of his prominence, his influence and his wealth. Various false charges were trumped up against him because of the powerful opposition he exerted against the war. He was accused of being a Tory, of being in league with the enemies of the country and of giving comfort and aid to them. He was charged with disloyalty to the government and the violation of its laws.

On one occasion a body of men came to his house in the night, took him out of bed, scarcely giving him time to dress himself, hustled him off to the army camp where various false charges were preferred against him. Then under a charge of disloyalty he was marched off to military headquarters. Those who had him in charge took away his clothes. One took his shoes from off his feet, another took his hat, another his coat, another his shirt and trousers and gave him in place only such filthy rags as would hardly cover his body. They cut off his hair and beard and painted his body in black and red.

Visualize this picture if you can—Eld. Christopher Sower, one of the leading citizens of Pennsylvania, a great philanthropist, educator, publisher, minister of the Gospel, benefactor of all with whom he came in contact, being marched off by the minions of the law bareheaded, barefooted, with scarcely clothes enough to cover his body, treated like a malefactor, a criminal, a villain of the deepest dye. The shamelessness of it all reminds us of the injustice with which a wicked rabble maltreated the Christ. But Bishop Sower, like the Master whom he imitated, when reviled, reviled not again.

But this is only a small part of what Bro. Sower had to suffer because of his religion. When he had walked until he was almost exhausted from hunger and fatigue, being prodded on by the merciless bayonets of the soldiers, he finally met in the road a gentleman who knew him. This gentleman distressed at his plight offered to give him his shoes and hat if the soldiers would allow him to wear them. They promised, but in a little while other soldiers came and took these from him also and he was again destitute. General Muhlenberg, an old friend of Sower, heard of the outrage and immediately sent a note to General Washington requesting that he be released. This was done at once and the good man under an order from the commander-in-chief of the Revolutionary army was permitted to return to his home.

But this personal brutality was only the beginning of what the faithful elder of the Germantown church was called upon to suffer. He had scarcely returned to his home when he was attacked from another angle. This time his property was the goal. He was one of the wealthy men of Pennsylvania and of course his

splendid estate was a rich target for his enemies.
Branded as a disloyal and unpatriotic citizen, condemnation proceedings were started against his property.
His large house in which he lived, his splendid publishing establishment, well stocked with machinery and
supplies, his paper mills in which he manufactured the
paper for his presses, his ink factory, his type foun-
dry, his farms and other real estate, all were now
brought under condemnation. Writs were secured for
the seizing of this property and in clear violation of
the law this splendid estate was put under condemnation proceedings and sold, and the money appropriated
by officers of the government—and all this in the name
of patriotism!

But even this did not break the good man's heart.
Reduced almost in a day from affluence to abject poverty, this man of God lived on, never wavering in the
faith in which he had stood so consistently. But his
last years were full of sadness. It was only the consolation that he had in Christ, the sustaining power
of his faith in him, nurtured by a loving daughter and
other friends, that kept him from giving way to blank
despair.

To the end he remained a faithful, noble leader of
the little body of members at Germantown. His example of fidelity was a great inspiration to the distracted church of his day. To show how the church
appreciated his loyal example he was appointed by
Annual Conference, a few years before his death, to
visit the congregations of Pennsylvania, to bring them
messages of courage, of hope, and fidelity, and to

assist them in the reorganization of their church establishments by the ordination of elders, the election of ministers and other officers. So to the end he was the same noble godly man, the same wise leader, the same helpful counselor that he had been throughout his life. He died in 1784, not far from the place where he had spent his eventful life. His last days were filled with extreme sadness. Despoiled of his wealth and reduced to poverty, he left Germantown in 1780, an old and broken man, and went to live with his daughter, Esther, who was married to Christopher Zimmerman and lived some twelve miles west of Germantown near the Methacton church. This church, a place of worship of the Menonites, is a short half mile from the village of Fairview and just north of Norristown. Here, with those who loved him, he made his home until death claimed him four years later. His body was laid to rest in the quiet cemetery of the Methacton church, which is kept in good repair to the present day. A suitable headstone marks his resting place.

There is another phase of this story without which the picture is not complete. We have seen that, as a rule, the Brethren stood true to their principles of peace and suffered every sort of injustice and persecution rather than violate their religious convictions. But this was not quite always true. There was an influential minority of the church that found the persecutions stronger than they could bear. Unlike Bishop Sower who could endure heroically to the bitter end, they yielded, under pressure, to the powers that be, gave up the principle of nonresistance, withdrew from the church and cast in their lot with the party in power.

The most conspicuous example of this was the family of Eld. Christopher Sower. Sturdy and heroic as he was, his sons do not seem to have been cast in the same heroic mold. They wavered under pressure, were moved by public opinion rather than by principles of conduct. They were not of the martyr type that could lead in an unpopular cause, that could suffer and be strong.

The Germans generally, at the time of the Revolution, did not represent the culture attained by the English. Most of the Germans adhered to sects distinguished by the strictness of their religious practice and had now brought themselves under reproach by their opposition to the war. The Brethren were classed among these.

We need to remember that the sons of Christopher Sower were brought up in affluence, had received an English education, moved in the best society of the Pennsylvania metropolis and were closely associated wth the leaders in the business and social life of their day. Just what the motives were chiefly that controlled their action, it may not be possible to discover, but it is easy to see the ties that would be broken should they cast in their lot with the despised German pacifists when they themselves had grown into the cultured English society of the community.

At any rate the third generation of the Sowers renounced their allegiance to the colony, espoused the

cause of Great Britain, turned Tory, and allied themselves with the English army. At the same time they
renounced their allegiance to the Brethren Church and
joined themselves to the Episcopalians. During the
winter of 1777-78 while the British army occupied
Philadelphia, two of the sons of Eld. Christopher
Sower published a paper in Philadelphia in support of
the British cause. When the army withdrew the following spring they left with it.

The oldest of this family, Christopher Sower the
third, who had been associated with his father in the
printing business and was a skilled printer, leaving
Philadelphia with the British army, went to New
Brunswick where he became the royal printer of the
province. Later he moved to Nova Scotia where he
served as postmaster general under an appointment
from the British crown. He had married Miss Hannah
Knorr before the Revolution. His oldest son was
Christopher the fourth, in the direct line of descent.

The defection of Christopher Sower's sons was a
great blow to the church. It removed practically a
type of leadership that had given the church such
prestige and influence in its early history. Alexander
Mack the second, now growing to be an old man, had
been joint elder with Christopher Sower of the Germantown congregation and continued to lead the mother church. While a man of true culture, broad sympathy, a genuine poet and a true Christian leader, he
nevertheless lacked the strong and impressive personality of the Sowers. With the passage of the second
Christopher in 1784, the distinctive type of leadership

that had made the colonial church great and influential ceased to exist.

So the sum total of the effect of the Revolution on the Brethren Church was far-reaching and vital. It scattered the membership and brought them under completely different environment. In 1775 there were only three congregations outside of Pennsylvania, one in New Jersey, and two in Maryland; and of those in Pennsylvania, nearly all were east of the Susquehanna River. The migration started by the war removed from the Pennsylvania churches some of their strongest leaders. Others were discouraged and their spirits crushed. While the church as a body had weathered the storm of persecution resolutely and had stood true to its principles, it had emerged from the ordeal terribly weather-beaten, scarred and mangled, with its phalanxes scattered and its forces in tatters. It faced a new world under new conditions and with a new type of leadership.

CHAPTER XVII

THE CHURCH IN THE WILDERNESS

Our flashlight today falls on the church in exile. We have seen the Brethren, under the stress of war conditions, moving with their families and such belongings as they could carry with them in two tides of migration: one west, one south. By this means, in the four or five decades following the outbreak of the Revolution our Brethren formed settlements throughout western Pennsylvania and ran over into Ohio. Others moving southward left a string of settlements in Maryland, Virginia, western North Carolina, Tennessee, Kentucky, Indiana, Illinois, and crossed the Mississippi into Missouri. Here they located in the forests, on the prairies, in the river valleys; and generally with an instinctive and unerring judgment of the quality of soil they possessed themselves of some of the choicest sections of the various States into which they went.

In many of these communities, at the time of our story, the second or the third generation had fallen heir to the estate first acquired by the emigrants. In many instances the first cabin, hastily erected, had given way to a substantial and commodious farmhouse. Barns were already beginning to appear and other outbuildings for the protection of the stock and crops were evidences of prosperity. These seekers after liberty for conscience' sake had followed, through the years, one after another, or in little groups and were naturally led into communities where friends or relatives had already settled. In this way little Dunker communities gradually grew up in the several States.

In general the conditions of life in the different sections did not greatly differ. The emigrant, no matter what his occupation formerly had been, by the fact of his migration, almost invariably turned farmer. In Pennsylvania many of these Brethren had been tradespeople, shopkeepers, manufacturers, weavers, dyers, tailors, tanners and the like. But when they moved into new and sparsely settled communities, many of those who had formerly plied other trades became tillers of the soil; this for the good reason that there was usually scant demand for their former occupation and, in the place where they had gone, good land was to be had at a nominal cost, so that the best prospect for a prosperous and successful career lay in cultivating the soil. In this way, by about the year 1820, which is the time of our present picture, many of those who had left the Keystone State forty or more years ago, had now grown into prosperity. Many of them had acquired hundreds of acres of land, rich and productive, with an abundance of timber for fuel and buildings. They had equipped themselves with a substantial suite of farm buildings, had their farms well stocked with horses, cattle, sheep, hogs, chickens, and were beginning to feel comfortable and satisfied with their lot.

But the course of life that had led to this condition had been long and rough. The broad fields still covered with stumps were unquestioned evidence of the hard labor that lay at the foundation of their prosperity. There were as yet few roads and these in the spring of the year, sometimes practically impassable. There were no bridges over the creeks and rivers and the market for the farm produce was far away. Indeed it required a solid week for the farmer with his four horse team to market a load of wheat or bacon or potatoes and bring back the winter's supply of sugar, coffee and salt.

But the Brethren were prospering in their several communities. An approach to an average Brethren home at this time was an interesting experience. Back a mile from the main road the visitor approaches it through a narrow lane winding along the bank of a little creek on one side and a zigzag, crawling rail fence on the other. On the other side of the creek is a large strip of oak forest. On this side are fields enclosed by the everywhere present rail fence, some in pasture, some in wheat, some in corn, with the inevitable patch of flax and, sometimes, of tobacco.

In the pasture are seen fat horses and sleek glossy cows. As you come in sight of the buildings you will see other evidences of prosperity. If we have followed the tide of migration westward, a grove of trees will mark the location of the farmer's dwelling. If we have gone southward a natural cluster of oaks and some apple and cherry trees will be found near his abode.

As we approach the home we will find the farmhouse to be built of logs, stuccoed without and whitewashed within. It is a warm comfortable house. The small windows filled with a dozen tiny panes would look strange in our day. Of course there are more pretentious houses than this already; occasionally one of stone laid out with a great hallway and with beautiful grounds and gardens; but as yet our Brethren possessed few of these and we are trying to draw the picture of an average case.

Let us approach the house and what shall we find? Our brother and his good wife with their eight children give us a hearty greeting. The children are shy and bashful for they seldom see a stranger. But our brother receives us with a most cordial welcome. As a visitor we share the best of all that they have, and this with an unstinted liberality, because their entertainment is a service of love.

What will the visitor observe upon entering the house? He will find much of the furniture homemade, substantial and strong and serviceable rather than ornamental. Benches that the farmer himself has made, and these without backs, extend on both sides of the long table and serve the family at meal time. Simple hickory chairs are reserved for the best room, and a lone rocker is a luxury. The floor is made of broad pine boards sawed at the up and down sawmill over in the next county. The wall is covered with whitewash. You can not touch it without evidence of the contact. There are no pictures on the wall, no carpet on the floor. The great open fireplace which admits huge logs of wood serves both to heat the room in the long winter evenings and ofttimes to light it likewise. Rich pine knots are used for additional lighting, or perchance a tallow dip, or on rare occasions a tallow candle.

In a corner of the living room is the large spinning wheel used to convert the wool into yarn for the winter's clothing. In another room, or perchance in another building called the loom house, the great family loom is housed, where the wool from the sheep is converted into jeans for the men's clothing and into flannel for the women's dresses.

By the side of the large spinning wheel is a smaller one for the spinning of flax. A patch of flax is a well nigh indispensable part of any well regulated farm home. After pulling the crop, haggling the wood out of the fiber and preparing the tow for spinning, it is a part of the long winter evening's work for the women of the household to prepare the fiber for the loom. Then on the great family loom the flax is woven into linen for summer dresses, shirts, tablecloths, towels, bed spreads, pillowcases, and chaff ticks.

But supper is announced, and our guest is invited to the long table which occupies a corner in the kitchen. The meal has been prepared in iron kettles in the great fireplace. The bread was baked in great round loaves in an oven built in the yard near the back door of the kitchen. Each person is provided with a pewter plate and a wooden spoon. The meal consists of mush and milk served in earthen bowls, sliced bacon, potatoes and hominy, and, because they have company, jelly from the top shelf in the cup-

board.   Black coffee is served in blue earthenware
cups.

After supper the evening is spent in conversation
with the flax wheel humming merrily.   Our brother
is anxious to hear the news from another section.
They talk of the crops, business, politics, the church,
the home, the rearing of the children.   When the
grandfather clock in the corner announces the hour of
nine, the family with their guest gather around the
family altar.   A hymn is sung in German, a chapter
read from the New Testament.   The visitor leads in
prayer.   Then up the steep winding stairs to bed.

What of the children in this home?   We have said
there are eight.   Their clothes of homespun are made
in the family and the style for the children is not
materially different from that of the father and mother.   The children go to school two or three months in
the winter to the German pedagogue who teaches a
subscription school near the post office.   The rest
of the time they help with the work on the farm and
in the house.   On one Sunday in the month they attend
preaching at a neighbor's house some three miles away.
The whole family walks to the meeting and back.
They have no Sunday-schools or young people's meetings, so the other three Sundays of the month they
visit among their friends and neighbors.

The monthly preaching service which the family
attends is held in the home of the elder.   He is a son
of the elder who led the body of members to this place
forty years ago.   He has built a new house, a large

one, and he has arranged that the partition may be swung up and fastened so as to throw two large rooms together. Into this double room the Brethren and friends of the community are invited to come once a month for preaching. On the other three Sundays he has appointments in other neighborhoods.

The service begins at ten clock and closes about twelve. The meeting opens with a hymn from Ausbund. The minister reads two lines from the only copy of the hymn book present. Some brother raises a tune and all present join in the singing. Two more lines are read, and sung—and so on through the hymn. All kneel in prayer. The minister's petition is fervent and searching. At his request one of the deacons reads a chapter from the Sower Bible. The sermon is doctrinal and hortatory and covers most of the verses read. The exegesis is practical, the advice wholesome, the appeal strong, the effects evident. The audience goes away edified.

When the meeting is dismissed there is prolonged visiting. The greetings are cordial and fervent, the handshakes warm and hearty, and are invariably accompanied with the Christian salutation. These are glorious experiences in the community life.

No matter in what direction we have followed our emigrants, the foregoing will serve as a general setting for their life in the early twenties of the nineteenth century. But what does it mean for a church thus to go into seclusion? Veritably our Brethren had gone into the wilderness. Here they are establishing their homes, living their lives peaceably and thriftily. They are a frontier folk building up prosperous communities. They have not yet begun to build churches, but for two generations they have worshiped God in their own homes and in the homes of their neighbors.

They have prospered as families and as groups of families, but they have not mingled largely with other people. In fact the denominational tie is exceedingly strong. They marry almost entirely among themselves. The ministers of our Brethren, as was true of most other denominations, found it easy to point out the shortcomings of other Christian bodies. They believed profoundly in the way their fathers and grandfathers had worshiped. They did not inquire deeply into why they did thus and so. It was enough that their fathers and grandfathers had thus done.

The second and third generations of our emigrants had the scantiest educational opportunities. As a rule the boys learned to read and write and cipher. The girls sometimes attained the same accomplishments; more often they did not. There was no church paper and oftentimes the Bible was the only book in the house. If the family took the weekly paper printed at the county seat it was the exception and not the rule.

In their isolation these families naturally partook of their environment. This was narrow and wanting in beauty. Their homes contained little that appealed to the æsthetic sense. Pictures and music were almost unknown, except the hymns sung in meeting. The architecture of their houses, the layout of buildings and grounds, were planned, if there was any plan, from the standpoint of the practical rather than the artistic. Life was prosaic; it was severe, and hard and serious. There were few amusements, and recreation for its own sake was almost unknown. Life was earnest toil year in and year out.

Two leading ideas dominated the life of these pioneers. First, there was the idea of making a living and possessing a home. This was undertaken as a lifetime job. Get-rich-quick schemes were unknown among that sturdy population. If a young couple could buy a farm, clear off the timber, cultivate and develop the land, equip it with a substantial suite of farm buildings, and own it clear of debt at the end of life—this was an ideal to be worked for. Much more than this they did not expect; and if through the years they saw themselves approaching nearer and nearer this goal, they felt that they were reaching the object of their ambition.

This made life immensely earnest and serious, and it gave its stamp pretty generally to the Brethren of that day. They were an earnest, serious minded people. Life was an achievement. They were not satisfied to live from hand to mouth. They must acquire, they must accumulate. They could do this only at the expense of great personal self-denial. This they were willing to suffer. Their sense of thrift kept constantly before them the idea of acquisition. They were not anxious to spend lavishly on their homes or on their families; but they were anxious to pass on a certain tangible patrimony to their children. The possession of real estate was to them a mark of standing that designated them as substantial citizens of the community.

It was frequently true that our Brethren were among the best farmers in the neighborhood. In industry, in thrift, in economy, in the practical management of their affairs, our Brethren were looked up to and respected. But they kept away from the towns. They produced on the farm most of the things they needed for their households. They wove the jeans and linen for their clothes. They dried the " snits " and beans and corn for the winter's supply. The neighborhood mill ground their corn and wheat; and the smokehouse was always well stocked with hams and bacon and lard. They were good livers, none rich, none poor among them.

The other idea which played such an important part in the lives of our Brethren in their isolation was their religion. In all their vicissitudes they did not forget their religion. They took it with them wherever they went. Fortunately, in their migrations, they had gone for the most part in colonies and it was very frequently true that there was a minister among the emigrants or not very far away. These ministers were often men of splendid abilities and not infrequently they were possessed of sufficient means to make them economically independent, so that many of them, at the time of which we are writing, were already giving a good deal of time to breaking the bread of life to others.

Even where ministers were not to be found, or where isolated families or small groups of families found themselves for years without preaching services, they, as a rule remained true to their faith, read their Bibles, taught their children the truth as they understood it and brought them up in the ways of the Lord. There is reason to believe that in many isolated homes, even among the laity, grace at meals and the family altar were not forgotten. By these means religious convictions were kept alive and when perchance at a later time some minister might pass through the section, or locate within reach, here was already the nucleus of a church ready to hand.

It is not difficult to see what the church under conditions like this would be. Speaking generally, we should regard it remarkable, if a body of Christians who had thus buried themselves in the wilderness should have had a large outlook on life. The things needing attention right at home were too pressing, too important to give much opportunity for large plans in the interests of others.

Yet I think there was no time when the Church of the Brethren was not truly missionary in spirit, when there was not a real desire to help others, to lead them into better ways of life, to minister to their needs. This spirit, I take it, was ingrained in the very genius of the Brethren Church in all its history, and the church at this time, as in all the other periods of its history, found the way to express itself in helpful service on many occasions.

So if we keep these two ideas in mind, the earnest practical desire to get on in the world, to own property, to live independently, to leave their children a better competence than they started life with; and then the other desire, to be a good neighbor, a good friend, a helper in time of need, in material or in spiritual ways—in these two respects we can summarize the character of the Brethren Church as we see it groping its way by instinct, by the intuitive sense of what is right and good and the innate desire to live up to a certain standard of life that they have set for themselves—in these things we see the genius of the church in exile.

What shall we say of those congregations back in Pennsylvania that had not migrated? In some respects, at the time of our picture, their condition is decidedly superior to that of those who had gone away. They are better established, have better homes, are closer to market. But they too are distinctly rural churches, and after the distractions of the Revolutionary War and the passing of that great group of pre-Revolutionary leaders, their condition does not differ greatly from that of the average Brethren community.

After the death of the second Alexander Mack in 1803, city churches ceased to play a leading rôle among the Brethren. There are still leaders who embody something of the greatness of the earlier days, such as Peter Keyser of Philadelphia, the Prices at Indian Creek and at Price's Creek, the second Martin Urner at Coventry, and others; and they continued to give to their churches something of an afterglow of greatness that reminds us of the colonial church.

But the Church of the Brethren has become a rural church, and the rural atmosphere pervades all its activities. It is intensely interested in its own affairs and does not look far beyond the horizon. It has settled itself in little groups of families in a dozen States from the Atlantic to the Mississippi. There are no railroads as yet, and travel is difficult and slow and expensive. There is little visiting except the purely local. Under such conditions each community has a tendency to settle down and crystallize into a type of living all its own.

CHAPTER XVIII

THE CHURCH TRANSFORMED

We left the church a generation ago a little body of less than ten thousand members widely scattered through a dozen States, in little communities frequently a hundred miles apart, slowly settling down and crystallizing into fixed habits of life. The thousand miles of territory from east to west, and an extent nearly half as great from north to south, together with the slow and difficult means of travel in that day made some of these communities almost as remote from each other as if they had been on two continents. It is not difficult to see, under such circumstances that the solidarity which they had enjoyed in its early history would necessarily be impaired. These isolated communities would develop a type of life peculiar to themselves.

I wonder if we can understand how this came about? By the middle of the nineteenth century, many of the Brethren were established on homesteads in some of the richest farming sections of the United States. In numerous instances these homesteads had been in the continuous possession of these excellent farmers for three and sometimes four generations. As life had been simple, and the Brethren had not formed the habit of spending much on their living, they lived frugally and economically, but well; and by 1850 many of them had excellent country seats, some with large brick or stone houses, or if built of wood, neatly painted and commodious. They had good barns, with other outbuildings, and there were many evidences of prosperity. The third of a century preceding the time of our picture had been a highly prosperous era. Generally speaking, crops had been good, prices were high, and farmers prospered.

By this time many of the older congregations had supplied themselves with church houses built with a large audience room and conveniences for the love feast. There was already considerable visiting from one locality to another in a given region, especially on love feast occasions. In order to accommodate these guests the lofts of the church houses were sometimes equipped with bedding for the entertainment of visiting members. The large attendance of visitors to the big meeting, as the love feasts were called, was just beginning. A generation later it grew until it actually taxed the housing resources of the community to entertain the guests and horses of those who came from a distance.

In this way the Brethren communities comprising a county or two came to be very much alike, and these communities were growing. The churches were active. They were pushing out their frontiers and establishing new centers. In fact, in some places, the centers that had formerly been a hundred miles apart had almost grown together. There was more time for church work than there had been for many years, and it should be said to the credit of the leaders of that day, that some of them eagerly sought the opportunity to give a good deal of time and personal effort to the upbuilding of the church.

These were prosperous years for the Church of the Brethren. While still largely local, the congregations within a given community, working chiefly among themselves and without much touch with the church at large, were animated by a fine spirit of loyalty to the cause and a disposition to labor in its interests.

So it was that strong Dunker communities were now to be found in a number of States. In eastern Pennsylvania, and farther west in Morrison's Cove, in Maryland, in the Shenandoah Valley of northern Virginia, in southern Virginia, in the Miami Valley, and elsewhere, there were communities where the Brethren were the leading farmers, possessing commodious church houses, and many of them well established on the best estates in the neighborhood.

Now the very fact of their prosperity helped to determine the type of their development. In the three quarters of a century since the first settlement of the Brethren in these sections, they found themselves substantially established as the original settlers. As a natural consequence, they were at the center of the community life. They were the leaders of custom in the neighborhood. They were prosperous and influential and were looked up to. Nothing was more natural than for them to consider themselves, and for their neighbors to consider them, as the natural leaders in neighborhood affairs.

Under these circumstances the thing happened that usually happens in such cases. The life of the community settled down to a monotonous uniformity. Conservative by nature and trained by generations of protest against conformity to the life about them, they naturally arrogated to themselves something of the dogmatism that finds satisfaction in a position of authority. In every community there was a group of leaders who stood very staunchly for what they believed represented the spirit and ideals of the church, and they were not easily moved from the position they had taken.

So it came about as a gradual process of development that the different neighborhoods grew more and more into fixed views of life, which crystallized into set forms, and these in time became intolerant of change. A visitor among the more thickly settled communities of the Brethren would have observed a great deal of similarity in each neighborhood. In the church services, in the form of the church houses, the arrangement of the furniture, and in many other respects, the congregations would have looked very much alike. By 1850 too the members of the congregation looked very much alike. The dress of the men, the wearing of their hair and beards, the dresses of the sisters with their aprons and capes and shawls gave them much the same appearance.

Now this did not come about so much by any sharply defined design as by a natural tendency of neighborhoods to reduce their mode of living to a common type. While the neighborhoods had much of sameness, the neighborhoods themselves were different. The shape of the bonnet, the cut of the cape, the form of the prayer covering, the style of the brother's coat and hat were usually clear indications as to the sections of country from which they came. These distinctions were strongly in evidence at the Annual Conferences and were frequently remarked upon. You could tell as far as you could see a brother whether he came from Pennsylvania, Maryland, Virginia, Ohio, or somewhere else. The same was true of the sisters. A monotonous conformity to a type had settled down upon a church.

Now this is a distinct change from the broad-minded, aggressive, far-visioned ideals of life set by the early leaders. Probably the best designation we can give to the church at the middle of the nineteenth century is to say that it is a transformed church. Externally and in its methods of work it is different from the Church of the Brethren at the beginning. Isolation and three quarters of a century of frontier life have modified not only its external appearance, but also its spirit.

It has lost its breadth of vision. It has lost aggressiveness. It has lost the cultural atmosphere that formerly surrounded it. And it has attained a plebeian commonplaceness that has robbed it of its former stateliness and dignity. But it has not lost its sincerity of purpose, its altruistic interest in men, or its missionary spirit. It is the aggressive church of the Macks and the Sowers and the Beckers, plebeianized and rusticated and permeated with the spirit of the frontier and the farm. So the Church of the Brethren is a transformed church, dominated by a different spirit, a different leadership, and it goes about doing its work in a different way.

Let us see if we can understand how the church came into this condition. We will try to make the matter concrete by referring to specific instances. Let us take the church's attitude towards one of its fundamental doctrines, the doctrine of immersion. The church has always taught and practiced immersion as the only form of baptism authorized by the New Testament. And it has always taught and practiced trine immersion.

There seems to be no doubt, however, that in the early history of the church, persons who had been baptized by single immersion and were satisfied with their baptism were received into full fellowship by the Brethren without rebaptism. But along in the twenties the church began to advise that in such cases it would, " be better that they should be baptized again in the true order." The question was before the Annual Conference of 1834 again and was answered in this way: " Considered that though it has been done before, still we believe that the best and safest way is to baptize them right and according to the proper order (as we believe) and that hereafter it should not be done otherwise." Thus the church disposed of the matter of receiving into membership persons baptized by single immersion. The church was gradually closing the door to its former practice.

But the matter of rebaptism does not end here. It was only four years later, in 1838, that the question of rebaptism was again before the Conference, but now the issue was different. This time the query was, " Whether persons who had been baptized formerly elsewhere with a threefold immersion could be received among us without baptism." Here is the answer: " Considered almost unanimously that when such persons are satisfied with their baptism, having been performed in the right manner, they may be received as members without baptism, yet with stating to them the order of the Brethren and the laying on of hands. If they should however desire baptism, it may be granted to their satisfaction." So in 1838 while the church had closed the door to single immersion, it was perfectly willing to receive into fellowship persons baptized by trine immersion by others than the Church of the Brethren.

Let us see what happened in ten years. In 1848 there was a query before Annual Conference like this: " Ought we to receive any person into the church without baptism, having been baptized by any other order of people?" Answer, " Considered that this Yearly Meeting advises to be very careful in this matter and give it as their unanimous conclusion that it would be better to admit no person into the church without being baptized by the Brethren." This advice became the rule of the church, and many who read these lines will remember that it has been only in our day that this rule was changed. So the church contracted its practice from setting its approval upon single immersion to the rejection of all baptism except trine immersion performed by the Brethren; and all this in one generation.

What was true of the thought of the church in regard to baptism was true in other respects. The church was crystallizing into a hard and fast manner of life, changing from a liberal to a dogmatic attitude in its practices.

The order of dress in the church came about in much the same way. There is but slight reference to dress as such in the records of the church during the first hundred years of its history. The Brethren always dressed plainly because they have always been a sensible, practical, serious minded people. But there is no reason to think there was an established order of dress until after the dispersion in the closing decades of the eighteenth century. When the Brethren left Pennsylvania, they went with the style of dress they were accustomed to at the time. This, generally speaking, was modeled after the dress of Penn and the Quakers which had also become the dress of the Mennonites, the Moravians and other religious sects.

At first, in their isolation the Brethren's dress attracted little attention, and no thought was given to it; but in time, as others settled about them and changes in apparel naturally came into use, there was a tendency on the part of some of the Brethren to adopt the new styles. The changes were deplored as following the fashions of the world. To prevent the church from this departure a form of dress was prescribed. It

was the form practiced by " the old Brethren." In-
sistence on this form is what gave us our dress question.

At first the issue seems to have been less a matter
of plainness than a matter of change. Any change was
attributed to pride and worldliness. Fixing a form of
dress was therefore a natural part of the church's settling down to a routine of formal observance in all
phases of its life. It established a form of dress for
the purpose of preventing change. When the hoop
skirt, the bustle and the high sleeves later came as
ornaments of woman's dress, the principle of plainness
also became a motive for protest against change. In
the main, our dress question was only a phase of a
general protest against doing like others do.

Let us see a little more specifically what kind of
matters the church was interested in along in the
thirties and forties. Here are some of the questions
that were important enough to come to the Annual
Conference: " How is it considered if members go
to the public election and vote?" Brethren were advised not to take any part in elections. Might a
brother be a sale crier? It was thought to be " unbe-
coming for a brother so to serve." The question of
Brethren keeping hotel or tavern was before the Conference of 1835. It was considered " entirely unbe-
coming for Brethren to do so." There is no intima-
tion that the Conference held that it was wrong to
engage in these things, but to do so was to conform
to the ways of the world.

The answer to a query about members sending their

sons to college was, " Considered not advisable inasmuch as experience has taught that such will seldom come back afterward to the humble ways of the Lord." The advisability of conducting singing schools in meeting houses was answered that, " Meeting houses are no proper place for holding singing schools." Whether it be right for members to take part in Sunday-schools was answered, " Considered most advisable to take no part in such like things." Even taking the temperance pledge was condemned by the Annual Conference of 1842, and the same Conference thought to deliver a temperance lecture was " not advisable for a brother." As late as 1844 the singing of the different parts as bass, tenor, alto were advised against. In 1849 the Conference advised against Brethren having their likeness or profile taken. Fine houses and furniture, sleigh bells, carpets, fashionable clothing were other things considered by the Conferences in these years and advised against. But this is enough, I think, to show the drift of sentiment leading up to the conditions of 1850.

The thought of the Brethren was against change in any department of life. The matter of dress was only a small part of a general system. The church was ossifying, crystallizing into a fixed order. An unchanging, unyielding rigidity was encrusting the church in all phases of its life. Any change was deplored. Life had become static.

Here is a transformation. It had come gradually and naturally. It was the result largely of an isolated environment and was not peculiar to the Brethren. It received exaggerated emphasis from them, however, because of contracted vision and lack of social contacts. So life among the Brethren in 1850 was chaste, severe, rigid, narrow, formal, simple, earnest, sincere. While living after a strict order and discipline, this was not true to the extent that the spirit of sweetness and true devotion, earnest piety, love, charity and a genuine missionary spirit ceased to be characteristic of the Brethren.

Such a church in 1850 had a mission. It was in keeping with many of the rural sections at that time. The Brethren could go among the farmer folk with their message and manner of life and receive a respectable hearing. And here is where they did their work. They were a distinctly rural people. They were uneducated. Many of them could barely read, some not at all. Much of the preaching was largely protest against worldliness and emphasis upon the peculiar doctrines of the church. They had little vision of world needs and a contracted view of the gospel message. But they were sincere and were content to live restricted lives. So they avoided the settlements, took the open country for their parish, and devoted their simple methods of work, with their simple messages of love, to the simple uneducated people of the countryside.

But just to think, what a transformation has taken place! In seventy-five years the church has been almost completely changed. The things that made it beautiful and grand and impressive and influential are gone. The church has assumed a different rôle. It shrinks from public gaze. It seeks the obscurity and seclusion of the country. It avoids the towns. It finds satisfaction in its simplicity and commonplaceness. It is a changed, a transformed church—the church that went into the wilderness and under the influence of primitive conditions is about to emerge with the flavor of the forest and the fields and the wilderness upon it.

But our picture is something of a panorama. We cannot see all of it from one point of view, so we shall have to reset our camera.

What we have seen is true of only a part of the churches of the Brotherhood, those that have kept in touch with the Annual Conference. A reference to the Minute Book makes it clear that during this period the Conference swung back and forth from Pennsylvania to Ohio and south to Maryland and Virginia. The churches in this group of States were quite generally represented at the Conference, and of course their practice was very much alike. Other churches from the farther outlying sections were sometimes represented at the Conference. But many of the most remote congregations were almost wholly out of touch with the workings of the church.

It is true, also, that in some of these far outlying sections some of the strongest, ablest and most active Brethren were pushing forward the borders of Zion in an aggressive manner. The Wolfes, the Hendrickses, the Gibsons, and others were marked examples of heroic self-sacrificing service for the Master on the wilds of the American frontier.

So there was an important and growing group of

churches along the western fringe of the Brotherhood that were not in harmony with the church that we have seen. These were the "Far Western" churches. They were growing up on both sides of the Mississippi River, in Illinois, Missouri and Iowa. The conditions pertaining to these churches we have considered elsewhere and will not repeat here. (See Chapter IV.)

We need only to add that the difference in practice of the two groups of churches was a matter of great concern. It was so important that the two bodies could not fellowship with each other. A query before the Conference of 1850 was answered by advising members not to fraternize with the Far Western Brethren. So, in addition to its ultra-conservatism, the church of 1850 was also a divided church.

This is not to be wondered at. Under the circumstances it could hardly have been different. The wonder is that the difference was not greater than it was. In the absence of a church paper for three-quarters of a century there had been no general means of communication among all the churches.

So the church of 1850 is a divided church at the same time that it is almost hopelessly in the ruts. It is a church groping its way in the dark, plodding blindly in quest of something better than it knows. The church in all its history had never been so helpless, so much in need of a Moses to lead it out of the wilderness. It had never been so restricted in vision, so disintegrated, so devoid of enlightened leadership, so little inspired, as at the middle of the nineteenth century.

CHAPTER XIX

THE CHURCH COMING BACK

In writing the preceding chapter I was not unaware of the fact that at the middle of the nineteenth century there were already indications of a new spirit appearing at various places in the Brotherhood. At that time, however, they were chiefly indications, evidences of dissatisfaction with existing conditions, inclinations to try something different from what had been current, a desire for a broader outlook on life and a determination to do individual thinking.

It is significant that these indications came from widely remote sections of the country; in fact they represented all sections into which the Brethren had gone. The new spirit was showing itself in such men as John Kline and B. F. Moomaw of Virginia; Daniel P. Sayler of Maryland; James Quinter, Isaac Price, John Wise of Pennsylvania; George Hoke, Henry Kurtz, John P. Ebersole of Ohio; John A. Bowman of Tennessee; Hiel Hamilton and John Metzger of Indiana; Daniel B. Sturgis of Illinois; and among the Far Western Brethren by George Wolfe, Isham Gibson; and of course there were others.

So all over the Brotherhood a new life was beginning to work. This new spirit did not manifest itself in any one form, nor did it appear in the guise of a reformation movement. For the most part it was unconscious. It was a stirring in the souls of a younger generation for something that the church life of that day did not provide.

It is not easy to analyze what was going on in the hearts and minds of these brethren. They did not know themselves, but they were true to their finer feelings and responded to the impulse of their hearts to lead out in this way and that and give expression to a soul prompting that they could not deny. The forms in which they were led to act were as various as the sections from which they came. Notwithstanding the diversities of form in the various sections as the years came and went, one thing became perfectly clear: All over the Brotherhood there were signs of discontent with the ecclesiastical order and the church was looking out to a broader and clearer horizon. In other words, the church was beginning to come back.

In order to see more clearly just what these indications purported, observe the forms of their manifestation in a few typical instances. Among the rising generation of church leaders were men of large view and independent thought, men interested in the study of nature, especially of plants, and these particularly in their relation to medicine. Among these were practicing physicians as John Kline in Virginia, John Forney in Pennsylvania, Daniel B. Sturgis of Illinois, and John Wise of Pennsylvania, later of Kansas. These men were clear thinkers and they applied the methods of thought used in the study of science to the study of their Bibles. They represented a new type of biblical interpretation from that which had generally pre-

vailed among the Brethren for two or three generations. These just mentioned were able expounders of
the Word and gave themselves unstintingly to the dissemination of the gospel truth as they understood it.

There were also among the younger generation a
number who were especially gifted as evangelists, with
genuine powers of eloquence and the ability to move
men in a large way. Among these were D. P. Sayler
of Maryland, who, after his election to the ministry,
devoted himself to his high calling with such earnestness that in the first three months of his ministerial
labors a hundred young people were baptized into the
church. James Quinter was another of these. Being
anxious to serve the church in the largest way within
his power, he moved to Fayette County, in the western
part of Pennsylvania, where there was only a small
body of members. Under his able preaching, in the
first six months of his pastorate, he received sixty
persons into the church by baptism. In the northern
part of Ohio John P. Ebersole moved into the neighborhood where the Rome church is now located.
There were only a few scattered members in the community. He began to preach and devoted himself with
such diligence to his gospel ministry that in a few
years he had a flourishing congregation of more than
two hundred members. This is the type of work that
was beginning to appear in many sections of the Brotherhood.

In Virginia, John Kline and Benjamin F. Moomaw
were engaged in an extensive type of horseback evangelism. Brother Moomaw, from his home in Botetourt

County, had opened a number of preaching places comprising two or three counties, where, in the years that have followed, there have grown up some half dozen strong congregations. John Kline's travels were even more extensive, leading him into a number of States, on several occasions as far west as Indiana. He gave himself up almost completely to his great mission of horseback evangelism and it was not infrequent for him in his busy life to travel more than six thousand miles a year on horseback in this work.

In Illinois Dr. Daniel B. Sturgis was carrying on work of much the same type, traveling extensively on horseback and preaching the Gospel wherever opportunity afforded, healing the sick, advocating in public debates the principles of the church he represented, and carrying on an extensive epistolary correspondence; a persistent worker who left a deep impress on his generation. Farther west still, on both sides of the Mississippi River, George Wolfe, Isham Gibson and others were waging a ceaseless warefare upon the forces of evil in that new land. With discouragements and difficulties to encounter such as were unknown even in other parts of the Brotherhood, these resolute, sturdy pioneers of the cross laid broad and deep the foundations of the Brethren Church on the frontiers of the American wilderness.

Yes, there could be no question that the church was beginning to reach out again for some of those fine things in its past life that it had, for the time being, lost. The church was coming back. And it is significant that most of the things in which the new generation was expressing itself were in keeping with ideals that the church had fostered in its early history: so that the new life manifested in the church was not something wild, sensational, extraneous, or foreign to the Church of the Brethren. It was a revival of the ancient spirit with which the church had started and in some instances the new expression was almost in identical terms with that of the early church.

Let us see what were some of the organized forms in which the new spirit expressed itself. In a quarter of a century the church leaped forward into renewed activities with a vigor that is almost startling. The revival of Sunday-schools brought it back to the rich heritage of its colonial experience. The thirst for higher education was breaking out at many places, and the church was busying itself to supply the need. A church press could not longer be put off. Missionary activity of a new form was also beginning to knock at the door. It was felt that individual activities did not meet the whole demand of the Gospel. The church as an organization could not delegate its responsibility for the preaching of the Gospel to the entire world, to those of its ministers who were willing and able to heed the call.

There were various sections in the Brotherhood too where the most intelligent members and most independent thinkers were not satisfied with certain usages that the church had gradually drifted into since its dispersion. These were for the most part matters pertaining to the observance of the love feast. They felt that the church had departed from the usage of the founders, and so thoroughly were they convinced that they were right that they kept up a ceaseless agitation of the matter, although generally in a beautiful Christian spirit.

These and other manifestations that might be cited were indisputable evidences of a new life in the church, a new vision in its leaders, a clear indication that the church of the new day was anxious to reincorporate into its usage and practice numerous things that it, in its frontier experience, had lost.　The church was beginning to read its Bible anew with an increased intelligence, with a clearer understanding of its mission, with a new conception of its responsibility as a Christian body before the world.　The church was coming back.

We can probably best understand what was going on by selecting a few of the most outstanding lines of church activity and see in a little detail how the church was struggling to express itself through these.　Take first the revived interest in Sunday-schools, in which the church had played such a glorious part a hundred years before.　Following the dispersal at the time of the Revolutionary War it seems that Sunday-schools had fallen entirely into neglect for several generations. This seems a little strange in view of the fact that the Pennsylvania churches, in close contact with the mother church at Germantown, had not changed in any way commensurate with the churches that had migrated into the wilderness, yet here too Sunday-schools for at least fifty years seem to have been entirely unknown.

Probably this strange condition can best be understood by remembering that the Pennsylvania churches were among those regularly represented at the Annual Conference and that gradually the church as it expressed itself through the Conference came to discourage Sunday-schools and later to oppose them. But it is also significant that the first revival of interest in Sunday-schools came in these same Pennsylvania churches.

The first Sunday-school in this revival, in which the Brethren seem to have had a part was organized in the Oley congregation in Pennsylvania as early as 1832. The thing that brought about the opening of this Sunday-school was a sudden exodus of many of the families of the congregation which left the membership without a resident minister, and the group was so small that they were not able to provide preaching services. Under these circumstances, in order not to be wholly deprived of religious services, the congregation joined in a union Sunday-school held in a schoolhouse in the neighborhood.

It was in 1845, however, that the first Sunday-school appeared among the Brethren under normal conditions. This was organized at Manheim, Pennsylvania, by Hiram Gibble. It was a union school and met in a log schoolhouse not far from the Manheim church.

Doctor Henry Geiger was elected to the ministry in the Philadelphia church in 1853. He hesitated to accept the call on the ground that it was against the usage of the church to have Sunday-schools and he felt that his ministry could not be successful without the aid of the Sunday-school in the nurture of the young people. Accordingly the whole matter was taken under consideration by the congregation, and the result was that he accepted the ministry and the congregation gave him the privilege of organizing a Sunday-school. He became the first superintendent, and this Sunday-school has been in continuous existence from that day to this, a period of more than three quarters of a century. This is doubtless the oldest Sunday-school in continuous existence among the Brethren today.

The Buffalo Valley church in Pennsylvania organized a Sunday-school in 1856 in which J. G. Royer was one of the teachers. This was also a union school and was held in a schoolhouse.

The same year another Sunday-school was started in Mifflin County, Pennsylvania, a few miles from Lewistown. When I was a student at Mt. Morris College in the early nineties I heard Eld. Joseph Amick tell about the organization of this school. He was a young man then, one of the prime movers in the matter and not yet a member of the church. He said that by a sort of mutual understanding word was passed around in the neighborhood that a Sunday-school would be organized at the schoolhouse on a certain Sunday afternoon. When the hour arrived at least a hundred young people had assembled. They naturally desired to open the Sunday-school with prayer, but when they canvassed the crowd there was not a single member of church present; so they had to proceed without a religious service. They organized the young people into classes somewhat according to age and used the New Testament as a text book. The school was held at the schoolhouse and was at first a union school. Young Amick and others especially interested tried to get some of the Brethren to go with them and superintend the school, but no one would undertake to do so. It was the general usage of the church then not to have Sunday-schools, and the ministers and deacons, while not necessarily opposed to Sunday-school, would not take part for fear of giving offense to those who were opposed. So a Lutheran minister was secured to superintend the school for several years. It was a Brethren community, however, and most of the young people were from Brethren families. After two or three years the way opened for the Brethren to take charge of the Sunday-school and it gradually came to be a Brethren school. In a short time nearly all of those who had part in it were received into the church.

Some years later, in 1865, a Sunday-school was started at Hoffer's meeting house in Dauphin County, Pennsylvania. Brother William Hertzler, father of Eld. S. H. Hertzler, was the first superintendent. This Sunday-school was held in the church and seems to hold two distinctions. It was the first Sunday-school to be organized in what is now the Eastern District of Pennsylvania and was the first, except in Philadelphia, to be held in a Brethren church.

Three years later, in 1868, another Sunday-school was organized at Green Tree and this also was held in the church.

So it was natural, I think, that in these Pennsylvania churches which had been less affected by migration than other parts of the Brotherhood should revive the former practice of the church in establishing Sunday-schools. From these scattered beginnings, the Sunday-school cause grew and flourished, so that by 1875 Sunday-schools were beginning to appear in almost all sections of the Brotherhood. In Sunday-school work the church was coming back.

Let us look briefly at the revival of the publishing interests in the church. Since the Revolutionary War the Brethren had had but little to do with printing. Now and then one or another had issued a book or pamphlet, as for instance, Benjamin Bowman of Virginia, who printed a little book that had a great deal to do with bringing Peter Nead into the Church of the Brethren. It was in 1850 that Bro. Nead published his book, " Nead's Theology," of four hundred and seventy-two pages, having issued parts of the same material in several separated publications before. Henry Kurtz in Ohio was printing German school books and other things.

But there was no periodical published by the Brethren for seventy-five years when Henry Kurtz began in 1851 to issue the *Gospel Visitor* from the loft of his spring house near Poland, Ohio. This undertaking was begun with the greatest caution. A query to the Annual Conference of 1850 recommended that the matter be studied for a year before any thing be done. The Conference of 1851 reluctantly gave permission to make the venture. The monthly *Visitor* began to appear in April with a subscription list of about three hundred. Many were still afraid that a paper would make trouble in the church; but Eld. Kurtz, who knew the spirit of the church well, was tactful and persevering and he gradually won the confidence of the people so that his enterprise was allowed to stand or fall on its merits. At first Bro. Kurtz did not only the editing but wrote most of the copy. His editorial office was the sitting room of his farm house. When set in type the pages were run off on a hand lever press located in the spring house loft. Then the edition was hauled over mud roads, sometimes practically impassable, five miles to the rural post office. A man with less nerve and perseverance than Bro. Kurtz would certainly have given up the enterprise, but not so the editor of the *Gospel Visitor*. He couldn't give up, no matter how much he may have felt like doing so.

He tells us in the first issue of the paper why he was impelled to start the *Visitor*. He knew the opposition it would encounter, and he knew the difficulties the enterprise involved, but when he felt like putting it off he was constantly confronted by one scripture that he could not get off his heart. That scripture is this: " He that knoweth to do good and doeth it not, to him it is sin." Brother Kurtz's enlightened vision told him that the church needed a paper and that vision haunted him day and night until it was put into effect. Like the great apostle, he was not disobedient to the heavenly vision.

After carrying the burden almost alone for five years the editor, in 1856, induced James Quinter to become a partner with him and associate editor. This relieved the veteran editor very much. Gradually too the paper was winning its way. More and better manuscripts were secured from other contributors and as the years went by the paper got more and more firmly on its feet and found a fixed place in the life of the church.

Thirteen years after the *Gospel Visitor* was started Henry R. Holsinger, who had learned the printer's trade in the *Visitor* office as a boy, started the *Christian Family Companion,* published at Tyrone, Pennsylvania. This was a weekly and was distinctively different in tone from the *Visitor*. The *Companion* was outspoken in its criticism of certain practices in the church and conducted an open forum in which contributors were invited to express their minds as they felt inclined to do. These opportunities were eagerly grasped and through the *Companion* a good deal of sharp criticism was launched against certain usages and customs in the church. Some of these no doubt deserved criticism, but as to how much good criticism will do depends a good deal on the spirit in which it is given. The criticism in the *Christian Family Companion* was not always in the most commendable spirit, and many, especially among the older brethren, were very much hurt at some strictures that appeared in its pages.

It was with the purpose of reacting against the free course of the *Companion* that the *Pilgrim* was started by H. B. and J. B. Brumbaugh at Huntingdon, Pennsylvania, in 1870. The Brumbaughs were probably as aggressive as H. R. Holsinger but they were much more tactful in managing their paper. They prevented harsh and cutting things from appearing in its pages and the editorial policy of the *Pilgrim* was constructive and helpful, and, it should be added, conciliatory.

It was in 1870 also that our first juvenile periodical appeared. This was entitled the *Pious Youth,* printed by H. R. Holsinger at Tyrone. Evidently the interest of the church in reaching the various groups within her borders was being sought out. It was about the same time that the Brumbaughs at Huntingdon began to issue the *Golden Dawn,* a monthly magazine artistically gotten up and manifesting a beautiful cultural spirit. It was designed to cultivate the spiritual side of the young people of the church. It was one of those magazines of which we sometimes hear it said, it was too good to live. In other words, the church was not ready for it. It was discontinued at the end of the first year. 1870 was a fruitful year in the launching of publications. It was during this year also that the *Vindicator* was started by Eld. Samuel Kinzie of Dayton, Ohio.

So in less than twenty years after the *Gospel Visitor* appeared we had six periodicals in the church, each bidding for the patronage of the membership. It is evident that as regards publications the church was coming back.

In regard to higher education also the church began to show a changed attitude about the middle of the century. Even before this some of her leading members had already entered the field of teaching and had met with conspicuous success. In preparation for this work some of them had attended normal schools or special schools for the preparation of teachers, and had thus come in contact with higher culture. There had been rash spirits also who had ventured into the colleges and universities with the avowed purpose of drinking deeply at the Pierian Spring.

Of these latter some were not willing to return later to the restricted confines of their bringing up and so found themselves out of harmony with the church life they had known. These were frequently lost to the church and sometimes to Christianity. In was probably a recognition of this fact as much as any one thing that brought about a changed attitude of the church in regard to higher education. It was evident that if the church did not provide the means of educating her young people she must expect to lose many of them from the church. This conviction seems to have seized the church somewhat definitely around the middle of the century. We are not surprised, under such conditions, that a people like the Brethren, to whom their children have always been their most precious possession, should be casting about to find the means for saving them.

Jacob Miller, of Buffalo Mills, Pennsylvania, was probably the first to tackle this question in a practical way. He had been teaching in the public schools of Pennsylvania for several years and with unusual success. The thought now came to him, and it was probably suggested by others also, that he give his splendid abilities to the special work of educating the young people of the church. To do this he erected at his own cost, in the summer of 1852, a building for the purpose. It was a large structure, as school buildings went in that day, being about 36 x 50 feet. It was built for a growing institution. He opened its doors to the public in September. Besides a large patronage the school enrolled a number of persons from a distance. Young men and women came to share its advantages and boarded with the family. It was in every way a success and showed the thirst of the young people of the church for superior educational advantages. The school, however, was destined to enjoy only one happy, prosperous year. Towards the end of the session, in the spring of 1853, Bro. Miller's health gave away, due chiefly to overwork. He rapidly declined and died, and his splendid project came abruptly to an untimely end.

But the new spirit was not dead. A few years later it manifested itself in Rockingham County, Virginia, near Broadway. Here in the fall of 1857 a group of leading brethren met to consider how they could improve the educational facilities for the young people of the neighborhood. They decided that they could best provide for them by building a private school, which was to be known as the Cedar Grove Seminary. This they proceeded forthwith to do. I remember this building well, which was rather an imposing structure and considerably larger than any public school building in the vicinity. John Kline, John J. Bowman, and Daniel Miller were leaders in the movement, the latter two being laymen.

These two schools, at Buffalo Mills and at Broadway, were strictly of the academic type. They gave work considerably in advance of the public schools of their day but restricted the curriculum to English subjects.

A third venture was made in Mifflin County, Pennsylvania, in the spring of 1861, when S. Z. Sharp bought the Kishacoquillas Seminary and made it a Brethren school. He ran the school for five years. It enjoyed a good patronage and extended the curriculum to include the higher mathematics, foreign languages and the sciences. It prepared for the colleges of that day and added the freshman year of the college course.

In the fall of the same year at New Vienna, Ohio, the New Vienna Academy was opened by James Quinter and others. The school was conducted for about three years when it had to be closed for the lack of support. In this school too the course was planned to meet all requirements for college entrance, the foreign languages, the sciences and mathematics being included in the curriculum.

From the academy to the college was a natural step and this step was the next the church determined to take. At Bourbon, Indiana, a college had failed. As there were many Brethren in that section of the State a general feeling seemed to prevail among them that they should secure this property and provide suitable educational opportunities for their young people. A query to this effect was brought to the District Meeting in 1869 and approved by an almost unanimous vote.

So the property was bought, extensive improvements were made, a faculty employed, and preparations concluded to open the school in the fall of 1870. The school was to be known as Salem College. Oliver W. Miller was chosen president. The school was extensively advertised and represented as being equal to the best colleges of the country. On the opening day a good student body was present and the work started hopefully. During the first session, however, vexing problems insisted on thrusting themselves upon the administration. The second year there were more of these and they seemed to increase with the years. The church had spent a good deal of money in improvements before the school was opened. These improvements had been made chiefly on borrowed money, and the debts did not decrease during these early trying years. So after a heroic effort to establish a college, after four years the promoters of the enterprise were compelled to give it up and the property reverted to its former owners.

It was in 1872 while Salem College seemed to be a going concern that some of the Brethren in western Pennsylvania decided that they must have a school for the development of their young people. A committee appointed for the purpose selected Berlin as a suitable location for the school. They also had big plans for a real institution of learning. One of these was that they would raise a hundred thousand dollars for the erection of buildings and for the support of the institution before they opened its doors. This they tried earnestly to do. Solicitors were put into the field to raise the money, but all they could do after two years of the most earnest solicitation was to show a subscription list aggregating about sixty thousand dollars; so the school never materialized. It was clear that the church was not yet ready to support education on this scale.

It was during this same quarter of the century that J. G. Royer developed a normal school at Burnettsville, Indiana, which enjoyed unusual success for several years. And it was in 1874 that Howard Miller and Lewis Kimmel began another normal school at the Plumb Creek church near Elderton, Pennsylvania. In fact they used the church as a schoolhouse. This fact is significant and is indicative of the Brethren's idea of higher education. Education was to be a handmaid of the church, and all of this early effort on the part of the Brethren to provide schools was with the one idea that they might develop their children and make them better Christians, better able to do the work of the church in the world.

So the church in a very definite way was reaching out after the liberalizing power of education which had played such a conspicuous part in its early years. As regards higher education, the church in 1875 was definitely coming back. In a short period of twenty-two years eight separate efforts had been made to establish schools, more than an average of one for every three years. Certainly as regards education the church was coming back.

In this survey we cannot avoid a brief look at

the church in relation to the missionary enterprise. Of course the Church of the Brethren at no time in its history had supported what we call today foreign missions, that is, missions to heathen people. But in the early history of the Brethren no other denomination was doing so. It will be recalled that the modern missionary enterprise, as we know it, began in the early years of the nineteenth century. Through all of their history, however, the Brethren have been distinctly and positively missionary in spirit and in practice. Their mission fields always lay adjacent to them and there was never a time in their history when they did not, according to their ability, manifest a commendable zeal in carrying the Gospel to those about them.

It is significant that it was just about the middle of the nineteenth century again that a definite effort to promote the spread of the gospel by the Brethren was earnestly urged. A query raising the question as to whether the church should not be more actively engaged in preaching the Gospel was before the Conference of 1852. This Conference agreed that more work of this kind should be done but took no action in reference to the matter.

Four years later, in 1856, a query was again presented to the Conference urging that something be done so that the recommendation of 1852 should not be a dead letter. The Conference again put its approval upon the endeavor and encouraged the Brethren in their personal activities.

Two years later a plan for organized missionary

effort was laid before the Conference. Evidently somebody had been thinking deeply and seriously upon the matter. In brief, the plan proposed the following: that States in which there were a considerable number of Brethren should form themselves into Districts; that Districts should hold District meetings; each District should have a District treasury, to which the churches should be asked to contribute; the District should appoint two or more of its ministers, such as would be willing to go, to travel as evangelists through the outlying territory of the District for a year: the District was to pay their expenses and to provide for their families in their absences.

This was a plan for evangelism on the basis of State Districts. The Conference did not see its way clear to pass the query, but it went on record as believing that the subject was " worthy of serious and prayerful consideration."

A query to the next Conference urged the passing of the paper the year before, affirming that there were many places in the Brotherhood where Brethren were anxious to see the church more active in the spread of the Gospel. The meeting, however, refused to pass the measure, but recommended it to the Districts and gave permission to any District to put it in operation within its territory. At the same time the Conference appointed a committee of six elders to bring a report to the next Conference which would provide a plan by which the measure might become operative for the entire Brotherhood.

The committee came back next year with their plan worked out. On the basis of what had been considered before, the committee now recommended that in support of the District treasuries the churches be asked to take up weekly offerings; that each congregation appoint a delegate to the District Meeting; that the District Meetings use the funds in the District treasury "as they shall judge most conducive to the glory of God and the salvation of souls." Further, each District Meeting was to send a delegate to Annual Meeting and this delegate was expected to make a report of the District work to the Conference. In this way all the activities would head up in the Conference.

After making this report in the early summer of 1860, the Conference decided it would be unwise to adopt it as a general rule of the church. This decision was due to the fact that the Conference was very poorly attended. It was held that year at Bristol, Tennessee, and it will be remembered that the Civil War had already begun and that there was much excitement and confusion and turmoil, both North and South. So the matter was allowed to rest and for the next half dozen years there is no record that the matter was further considered in any of the Conferences. The church for the time being had its hands full of more immediate problems.

It was in 1868, however, that the plan of 1860 was finally adopted by the Conference, but no effort was made to put it into operation for a good many years to come. It was a cumbersome plan, difficult to operate

no doubt, and it was not until 1880 that the church as
an organization actually stepped forward in a practical
way to do mission work. But there is nothing in all
this period of enlarging vision that indicates more
clearly the soul of the church reaching out after a
means of expressing itself in a larger service to the
world.

In this too the church was coming back. It was
feeling its obligations to its neighbors very much as
the infant church had felt it a hundred and fifty years
before in Europe, and later in America. It was coming back to those glorious ideals of its young life and
was yearning to express itself in service to the whole
world.

This survey must suffice to show that by the end of
the third quarter of the nineteenth century the church
was certainly coming back to the principles and practices and also the spirit of its early life. No matter
that it had not yet developed a workable plan for mission work, it was grappling in dead earnestness with
the subject. No matter that it had not yet produced
a school system that it could be sure would bring the
relief it needed, it was working with might and main
to meet its educational needs. The newly established
press was wielding a tremendous influence upon the
church, and Sunday-schools were showing their salu-
tary effects almost everywhere. The church was coming back to its ancient landmarks. Naturally it lacked
much as yet of the liberality and generous spirit that
distinguished the church in the colonial days, but it

was beginning to feel the same impulses and was begin-
ing to catch something of the same great vision.

It will be observed, of course, that what is here said
applies to the church as a body. As is well known
there was a group in the church at the time that failed
to see the new vision and did not feel the new impulse, and so refused to go forward into the larger
church life. These in time fell out of the ranks, but
the church was on its way to better days and a richer
religious experience.

CHAPTER XX

THE CHURCH WITH A WORLD MISSION

After the church began to free itself from some of the things it acquired during the wilderness period it made steady advancement for a period of thirty years. It was probably too much to expect, however, that it would move forward as a solid body to its complete liberation. As was natural under the circumstances, some parts of the body moved faster than others. As the years went by this discrepancy became all the while clearer; one part desired to move faster than the main body was ready to go, and another part wished to move more slowly, or not at all. Thus three groups soon merged into clear view.

From the very nature of the case these grew farther apart year by year. In a short time each extreme became so far at variance with the main body that coöperation seemed impossible; so, to the great sorrow of all, these extreme factions sloughed off leaving the main body a compact organic unity.

Here was a body of Christian people, approximately a hundred thousand in number, looking forward and upward and yet moving cautiously toward the light that beckoned from the distance. They were anything but radical and they were anything but lifeless. This body had caught the vision of a larger spiritual life. They had not yet mastered all the intricacies of its attainment, but they were looking forward with hope and assurance.

Their steady progress is marked by distinct stages along the way. For instance the two hundredth anniversary of the organization of the church in Germany, fittingly celebrated at the Annual Conference at Des Moines, Iowa, in 1908, was clearly indicative of a growing conception of the great mission and ideals of the founders. In the special program prepared for the celebration the whole two hundred years of the church's history was brought under review. The year that was taken to prepare the program gave time for thoughtful study of the church's career, which undoubtedly resulted in a clearer understanding of the ideals of the founders and of the present mission of the church. Two years later, at the first Conference held at Winona Lake, Indiana, there was a noticeable freedom of discussion which had not characterized the Conference in many years. Brethren who differed and differed radically, but honestly, expressed themselves with a fullness and freedom on the floor of the Conference that was new in Conference experience; and this was so marked that it was extensively commented upon. In some quarters it was hailed as a growing liberality and freedom in the councils of the church. In other quarters it was deeply deplored as a sign of waning authority on the part of older bishops and leaders and an increasing prestige of younger brethren. The next year the Conference of 1911 adopted a so-called dress report that had been several years in preparation and was looked forward to by all the elements of the church with a great deal of interest. This report made several distinct changes in the general attitude of the church towards the matter of dress, and these were in the interest of liberality. The passage of this report relieved a strong tension that had been noticed for a number of years. Gradually the freedom of discussion, a liberality of view, a charitable attitude of one toward another, the recognition of honesty of thought and conviction among those who differed in their ideas of church polity—these and other things gradually led to the attainment of a common viewpoint and made possible the forward march of the church as a body toward a larger vision of its mission and a fuller realization of its responsibility to the peoples of the world.

Probably we can see the significance of what was going on more clearly by looking into some of the activities of the church. In the last chapter we saw the church struggling to find a way to launch out in missionary work. Now without pursuing this story in detail we shall simply call attention to the fact that the church was gradually finding its way to carry out those noble impulses which were stirring deeply in the heart of the body. There was an earnest yearning to push out into the great field of world evangelization. The church felt the call to do so and felt it deeply. Yet always a conservative body, it refused to move faster than it saw the light. So while it was grappling with the problem an incident occurred that helped it forward in its work.

A young man from northern Europe, a seeker after religious truth, came to America in quest of a body of Christians who believed and practiced what he understood the New Testament to teach. He searched in various sections of the country for two years and finally came in contact with the Brethren in Illinois. He attended their meetings, visited in their homes, discussed with them the doctrines of the church, studied the history of the denomination, and in all important respects he found that his understanding of the gospel message was in substantial agreement with the faith and practice of the Brethren. He applied for baptism and was accepted.

This young man was a native of Denmark. His name was Christian Hope. He had left a father and mother and many friends in the home country. Naturally his thought went back to them. He had found the consolation of the Gospel for which his heart had yearned for many years. He was anxious that his friends might enjoy the same spiritual privileges that he enjoyed. He began to translate some Brethren tracts into Danish. He sent some of the Brethren's literature to friends in Denmark who could read English. Ere long request came from a young man to be admitted into the church. Under the circumstances Bro. Hope desired to go back and be a missionary to his own people. But how could this be done? The Brethren Church had no foreign mission, no organization by which it could carry on missionary work abroad. In Northern Illinois, however, the question was of such vital significance and of such gripping importance that a special District Meeting took the matter under advisement and decided to finance and execute a missionary enterprise to Denmark on its own account.

So it was that the first foreign mission of the church was organized and supported by a State District before the church as a body was ready to undertake the enterprise. This is indicative of the cautious spirit in which the church stepped forward into its great world mission.

In the course of time, however, the church saw its way clear to set up a mission board, receive contributions, find young people willing to dedicate their lives to service in the nonChristian world, and thus in commendable diligence it has planted missions in each of the greatest regions of spiritual darkness upon the globe. The mission to India was opened in 1894 and has grown until more than a hundred American workers have been assigned to this field. At least eleven stations have been developed and the largest congregation in the Church of the Brethren today is one of the India churches. The mission in China was opened in 1908, the two hundredth anniversary of the organization. This work too has grown in a most commendable way. Africa was entered in 1922 and already a great work has been wrought among the dark people of that region. In the prosecution of this work the church has been spending for many years approximately one third of a million dollars annually. There is no question about the church's world-wide vision of its mission to its nonChristian peoples.

At home, too, the church has strongly developed its

mission work. The whole field is now organized into about fifty State Districts in most of which aggressive work is carried on by the District organization. This work has been largely developed and improved in the last decade by the appointment of a home mission secretary who spends much of his time in the field studying conditions, collecting data, conferring with leaders and workers, finding strategic points for work, and organizing more effectively the forces on the field. This study is bringing to light the places where changes for the improvement of the service may best be made.

It is impossible to tell what moneys are spent by the Districts in this work, because much of it is done by the organized church forces, and largely without money compensation; but it is probably true that as much money is expended in the home fields directly as on the foreign field, and it is probably also true that as much service is given on the home field without compensation as is paid for.

So when we look at the church's mission activity its view is world wide. The church seeks not only to send the Gospel to the most needy sections of the most backward peoples of the world and to evangelize outlying sections in the home land, but it has opened work also among the foreign elements in our own country. This is true especially among the Mexicans along our southern border, and among Chinese, Italians, and other nationalities in our large cities. The church is thoroughly aroused to its opportunity and its duty to take the gospel message to all within its power, regardless of place, race, or other conditions. The church as regards mission work has a world vision, and it seeks to make this vision operative in a world mission.

In a former chapter we noticed briefly how education grew up among the Brethren and how they tussled with the question for years before they succeeded in establishing an institution that would be permanent. This persistent effort is indicative of the spirit with which the church has taken hold of the cause of Christian education. Following that early period of abortive effort schools soon began to be established that came to stay. From the numerous schools that were started almost wholly without plan, or any other consideration except the feeling of a local need, have come a half dozen or more high grade colleges.

In no great field of activity has the church shown itself more completely sold to an idea than in the development of these institutions of learning. It has left nothing undone within its power to equip its colleges fully in man power, in material resources, and in the maintenance of proper Christian standards. In the development of this educational program it has invested millions of dollars and is eagerly continuing its loyal support to put these institutions on firm financial footing. With limited means always and with strong competition with richer institutions, our colleges have gone forward winning their way in public esteem and efficiency in spite of their many handicaps. Several of them have been admitted into the educational associations in the territory where they exist, which places them on a par with the largest and richest and best administered institutions in the land; others are accredited by their respective state boards of education and other rating agencies and enjoy the favor of good patronage and the respect of leading educators in the States where they exist. There is probably no organized agency of the church to which the church has contributed of its resources with as an unstinted liberality and generosity as it has done for the maintenance of its colleges.

As a capstone, so to speak, of the church's educational system it has established and maintains a theological seminary, centrally located and adequately equipped. Bethany Biblical Seminary in Chicago provides a training center for the higher religious training of the church. To it are going an increasing number of the graduates of our different colleges year by year, young men and women who wish to prepare themselves for the larger work of religious teaching and leadership.

The attitude of the church towards evangelistic meetings is indicative of the change that was going on in the period we are now treating. Before the middle of the century prolonged evangelistic efforts were looked upon with suspicion, and branded as wild fire. A generation later meetings of this kind were beginning to be common in many parts of the Brotherhood, and the rapidity with which they came into favor along in the eighties and nineties had a tremendous effect upon the growth in numbers and the development of a new spirit in the church.

It is easy to see what a wonderful opportunity the

church had at this time. Hitherto it had been generally the custom that young people were hardly expected to join the church until they married and were ready to establish a home. So the conditions of the church at this time were just right for large ingatherings. In almost every neighborhood where the Brethren had churches there were large numbers of young men and young women, boys and girls, who were ready to respond to a cordial invitation to join the church. Consequently a series of meetings lasting two or three weeks would not infrequently result in an ingathering of forty or fifty young people, and frequently more.

It was only a short time, therefore, until the evangelists won their way in the confidence of the people and the dangerous fire from which some had shrunk was found to be nonexistent. Not only did these evangelistic efforts bring a large number of young people and some older ones into the folds of the church, but this very fact also wonderfully increased the spirit and life and activity of many of the congregations. So the last two decades of the nineteenth century was a remarkably prosperous period for the Church of the Brethren.

Of course this influx of the young people into the church naturally produced problems, problems of administration, problems of discipline, problems of spiritual nurture. Some of these problems the officials did not know very well how to deal with, and of course mistakes were made, naturally; in some instances by trying to deal with young people by the methods that had been current with heads of families, in some instances by the application of church machinery that was no longer applicable. But in time methods of church government and spiritual nurture were made to conform to present needs.

Since this turn of affairs towards evangelism, the preaching of the Word in series of evangelistic sermons has had a large place in the program of the church. Evangelism was the slogan adopted one year for the program of the Annual Conference. It was also the slogan for one year's effort in the Forward Movement Program, and that year was given first place in the larger activities of the church. Thus it is evident that evangelism has come to be one of the agencies through which the church has chosen to bring its message to the world.

In the field of social service the church was also beginning to feel a call to act. There were vast areas of underprivileged people that about this time seemed to claim the attention of the church; the slum districts of our large cities, for instance a field in which the church had never undertaken to minister. The church felt the call to lend a hand in bringing relief to the terrible conditions that prevailed there. It was along in the eighties or nineties when a small group of workers began work in the slums of Chicago. In Hastings Street a mission was opened. Street meetings were held, food and clothes were distributed, and some lives reclaimed.

A similar work was begun at about the same time in Brooklyn, New York. This was in an Italian settlement. This like the Hastings Street work in Chicago has been kept up to the present day. Bodies of members have been gathered and the cross of Christ established in these dark quarters. Similar efforts have been alike successful at other places.

The same impulse to social service led the church about this same time to establish a hospital. For many years the church struggled with an effort to build up a hospital in Chicago. The response on the part of the Brotherhood for funds to this end were not eagerly met. The matter dragged on for some years and was finally abandoned, but the effort is significant. The church was yearning for a means of asserting itself in a needy field of service which it had not hitherto used.

The purpose some years later to take an educational program of the church to a backward mountain region is an expression of the same social motive. It was along in the first decade of the twentieth century that the educational work was begun in a small way among the people of Greene County, Virginia, in the Blue Ridge Mountains. This grew gradually through the years until the General Mission Board of the church, through its home department, established a school and farm for the practical education of the people under a Christian environment.

The Greene County work was a practical effort to take the church and the Christian school to the people. The larger religious educational work of the church, functioning through the Sunday-school enterprise, was also growing and developing in a splendid way. To foster this work the church appointed an Advisory Board in 1911, whose business it was to encourage and help Sunday-schools in whatever way they found it advisable. The needs in administration, teaching, organization and other respects the board found to be so great that as an advisory body they felt themselves overwhelmed with the enormity of their task. As a consequence a few years later this board was dismissed and a board was elected with power and authority to exercise such oversight and direction of the Sunday-school work as the church needed. The board found itself with a great task upon its hands, but in the course of years it developed a program of operations, set standards, produced courses of teacher training, and has at length evolved a great system of schools of which the church may well be proud. The Church of the Brethren is one of the few denominations in this country in which the enrollment in Sunday-school continues to be larger than the entire membership of the church. Thus it is evident that the church has taken its place among the most aggressive champions of Sunday-school work in this country.

Naturally in this forward look of the church the church press played an important part. We saw in an earlier chapter with what vigor printing came back into the church after the middle of the last century. That enthusiasm continued. And the various printing establishments in the hands of the Brethren put forth a vast amount of literature in various forms. Suffice it to say that in the course of time the different periodicals merged gradually into one. By this means a unity of feeling in the Brotherhood and a spirit of coöperation among the churches was perceptibly felt. The details of this are reserved to its proper place. Here it is sufficient to indicate that the church was using the religious press as an agency for the furtherance of its mission not only at home but to the ends of the earth.

It is interesting to observe how its ideal of its mission in this respect grew. After sporadic efforts the church at length decided to establish a magazine for its young people. It had had years before this papers for children and for young people, but now it was striving for a higher class of journal. The new periodical was to be known as the *Inglenook*. This title was a happy stroke of ingenuity. It was suggestive of our German origin and the idea of a paper which the family could sit back in its easy chairs and peruse at pleasure. But what was a magazine for young people to be filled with? What kind of an intellectual ration was to be dealt out to them? The Brethren were suspicious of fiction, they were too practical and limited in literary appreciation to take kindly to imaginative stories; so here was an interesting experiment of trying to produce a magazine for young people solely out of factual material. But the Brethren have always had ideas of their own. They thought they knew what they wanted and went about getting it. They put into the enterprise the best they had in labor, ability, and editorial skill. The first editor was Howard Miller, one of the best writers and one of the most highly educated men in the Brotherhood. He gave the paper a distinctly personal touch. The second editor was Blanch Lentz, perhaps with the idea that a woman would find a way to win young people as readers. She was followed by E. M. Cobb whose travels abroad gave him a different outlook as an editor. Then came Henry M. Barwick, an enthusiastic college graduate, whose untimely death cut short his editorial career. Again Miss Lentz was drafted into service until S. C. Miller became editor. Finally it was voted to discontinue the magazine for lack of support.

A new paper was started on a different plan, a little more modest than the former venture. *Our Young People* was launched with the idea of making it appeal to the interests of young men and young woman, boys and girls. Fiction was no longer taboo. It had at length come to be known that imaginative stories may embody the noblest and finest truth. This paper has grown into a remarkable success. It is distinctly the most popular publication issued by the Brethren.

A publication of vast influence for many years was the *Missionary Visitor,* put out monthly by the General Mission Board and edited by one of its secretaries. Through its columns news and pictures from the foreign field went into thousands of homes. It enjoyed a large circulation because those giving a certain amount to missions were entitled to a free subscription on request. Since January, 1931, it has been merged with the *Gospel Messenger,* in the interest of economy and a wider reading of mission news.

Of course the representative periodical of the Broth-

erhood is the *Gospel Messenger*. This paper has had
a remarkable career. First, the property of a group
of interested Brethren who made it distinctively representative of the Brotherhood and thereby a powerful
unifying agency of the church, it has become the dis-
seminator of church news and religious teaching.
After being thoroughly established in the confidence
of the church at large generous stockholders and other
friends turned over this property in bulk as a free
gift to the church, the paper with its equipment being
valued at $50,000.00. Since that time the *Gospel Mes-
senger* has been conducted as the official organ of the
Church of the Brethren. Among religious weeklies it
holds high rank. Ably edited and covering all phases
of the church's interests, it deserves a place in every
Brethren Home. Through this agency the church
speaks its message to the world.

In the field of Sunday-school literature, the Brethren Publishing House also sends forth a body of literature of the first class. Here are helps for every
department of the Sunday-school, for teachers and
officers; also the graded lessons ably edited and well
printed.

The House has also entered upon the development
of church literature. It has printed numerous books,
chiefly by Brethren authors on a large variety of subjects; and gradually in this way is building up a church
literature, which will set the church right before the
world, let us hope, in many ways upon which there
has been much confused thinking. It is only recently
that a literary editor has been appointed to give special

attention to the development of this phase of our church literature. More and more the church is taking steps to bring its message, its life, its inspiration and influence, to the entire world.

The same disposition to reach out into the world at large is shown by the church's participation in inter-denominational coöperative enterprises. For a good many years the church has been represented on the International Council of Religious Education, with a member on the lesson committee. This is the commit-tee that chooses the international lessons for the Sun-day-school and develops the teaching plans for these lessons.

It has been active in the Anti-Saloon League. In fact when the matter of local option or state adoption of prohibition was under consideration, in many of the States, some of the leading workers in bringing temperance legislation to pass were our own Brethren. They have been alike active in anti-war work. Since the World War the Church of the Brethren has been one of the most active peace organizations in the United States. Coöperating with the Society of Friends and the Mennonites, the Brethren have made themselves felt in the dissemination of peace sentiment and opposition to war. In this as in many other ac-tivities the church has a world mission.

For many years the women of the church have been exceedingly active. Beginning as Sewing Societies and Missionary Societies, their work gradually developed into Aid Societies and these have more recently been further enlarged under the designation of Women's Work. In various ways the women have demonstrated their ability, not only to do things but to do them intelligently and well. They have been a powerful auxiliary in many phases in the work of the church: in raising money for the support of foreign missions, in providing clothing for the needy, in financing local building operations, in supporting home mission work, in local Christian teaching in the Daily Vacation Bible Schools, in furnishing rooms at colleges and hospitals, and in other ways. They have served nobly. Their contributions to direct enterprises of the General Mission Board alone reach a grand total of more than a million dollars, and doubtless their assistance distributed in many other ways is much larger.

A department of Men's Work has also been in process of development for several years. Organizations are being formed in many congregations of the Brotherhood, and some State Districts have been organized. These are great possibilities for usefulness in this movement that the church has not yet realized.

There are many other ways in which the church has reached out in the expansion of its activities. But further details are not necessary. The church come to the point where it has a pretty clear vision of its mission. And it seeks to translate this mission into terms of world service.